BALTIMORE TOWN AND FELL'S POINT

MARYLAND

DIRECTORY OF 1796

From the Original by THOMPSON and WALKER

With a Supplement Containing
Baltimore Naturalizations
1796-1803

by
Robert Barnes

HERITAGE BOOKS
2011

HERITAGE BOOKS
AN IMPRINT OF HERITAGE BOOKS, INC.

Books, CDs, and more—Worldwide

For our listing of thousands of titles see our website
at
www.HeritageBooks.com

Published 2011 by
HERITAGE BOOKS, INC.
Publishing Division
100 Railroad Ave. #104
Westminster, Maryland 21157

Other books by the author:

1783 Tax List of Baltimore County
Robert W. Barnes and Bettie S. Carothers

Baltimore County, Marriage References, 1659–1746

Baltimore County, Maryland Deed Abstracts, 1659–1750

Baltimore and Fell's Point Directory of 1796

Gleanings from Maryland Newspapers, 1776–85

Gleanings from Maryland Newspapers, 1786–90

Gleanings from Maryland Newspapers, 1791–95

Index to Baltimore County Wills, 1659–1850
Robert Barnes and Bettie S. Carothers

Index to Marriages and Deaths in the Baltimore County Advocate, *1850–1864*

International Standard Book Numbers
Paperbound: 978-1-58549-081-3
Clothbound: 978-0-7884-8660-9

THE 1796

BALTIMORE TOWN and FELL'S POINT

DIRECTORY

ABBOTT Andrew, grocer, 18, No. Howard st
ABRAHAMS Thomas, carman, Second, between Gay st. & the Falls
ACCLES Samuel, cordwainer, 57, South st.
ACKERMAN George, bricklayer, Old Town, 90, So. High st.
ADELAIDE Louissa, of St. Domingo, do. Low St.
ACKLAND John, cordwainer, do. 21, French st.
ADAMS William, Old Town, beyond Winen St.
ADAMS John, rigger, Exeter St. near the Causeway
ADAMS Bailey, carman, Eutau, So. of Baltimore St.
ADAMS Jacob, flour merchant, 21, No. Howard st.
ADAMS Alexander, cordwainer, Cow-Pen Lane.
ADAMS James, mariner, Fell's Point, Lancaster Alley, East of Bond st.
ADDERLEY Charles, Innkeeper, do. 26, Thames st.
ADOU Peter, store, Old town, 11, Bridge St.
AIKEN George, gold smith, and jeweller, 1, So. Calvert St.
AIKEN Andrew, druggist, 2, South St.
AIKENS Jeffry, labourer, Fell's Point, Strawbury Alley
AISGUITH William, Old Town, Wapping St.
ALRICKS Harmanus, mercht. dry goods and hard ware, 76, Baltimore St.
ALRICKS Harmanus, dwelling, Lemmons Alley
ALDRIGE John, mariner, Sharp St.
ALCOCK Joseph, tinman, 149, Baltimore St.
ALCOCK William, grocer, 61, No. Howard St.
ALLCOCK James, conveyancer, 13, Bank St.
ALLCOCK James, dry and wet goods store, Upper Water St.
ALLEN Catherine, widow, 45, No. Howard St.
ALLEN Michael, Innkeeper, Fell's Point, 36, Philpot St.
ALTER Christian, house carpenter, So. Howard St.
ALTER Frederick, carpenter, Fayette between Lib. & Ho.w'd Sts.
ALTER John, plaisterer, 24, No. Frederic St.
ALLISON Patrick, clergyman, East between Calvert and Gay St.
ALLENDER Joseph, physician, Fell's Point, 17, Thames St.
ALDERSON George,   do. 8, Shakespears Alley.
ALEXANDER William, taylor, Old Town, Albermarle St.
ALEXANDER Isabella, boarding house, 24, St. Paul's Lane
ALLFORD John, plaisterer, Old Town, No. Winon St.
ALLFATHER Henry, carpenter, King George St.
ALLVINE John, windsor chair maker, Caroline St.
ALE Christopher, butcher, Lee St. Federal Hill.
ALLMEN David, cooper, Triplets Alley.
ALHASFEN John Ernest, cordwainer, Hill st. Federal Hill.
ANDREW Maddox, dry goods store, 60, Baltimore St.
ANGEL James, Officer of the Reveune, 119, Baltimore St.
ANDERSON John and Henry, merchants, store and counting house, 12, Bowley's
wharf.
ANDERSON William, 52, No. Howard St.
ANDERSON Thomas, labourer, back of East St.
ANDERSON William, cooper, Triplet's Alley.
ANDREW and HALL, dry goods store, Old Town, Bridge St.
ANDREWS Nathan, soap boiler, do. Front St. opposite Baptist Meeting House.

AMOS James, dwelling, 58, Pratt St.
AMPHRIM François, of St. Domingo, Fell's Piont, Apple Alley, between Bond and Market Sts.
APPLEMAN Conrad, whip maker, 194, Baltimore St.
APPLEMAN Thomas, barber, Old Town, So. Green St.
APPLE Christian, waggoner, do. 30, French St.
APPLETON Richard, hair dresser, 17, Water St.
ARMOUR David, saddler, 48, South St.
ARNST Michael, labourer, No. side Lexington St.
ARMSTED Thomas, ship carpenter, Fell's Point, Wolf St.
ARMSTRONG James, do. Alisanna St.
ARMITAGE James, plaisterer, Sharp St.
ARMITAGE John, do. Eutau St.
ASHMAN William, dwelling, 102, Hanover St.
ASHER John, cordwainer, Carolina St.
ASH James, attorney at law, South side Second St.
ASKEW Jonathan, Innkeeper, 11, Market Place.
ASKEW Joseph, attorney at law, Fell's Point, 32, Market St.
ASKEW William, dry goods store, Old Town, 40, Bridge St.
ATRIDGE James, rigger, Fell's Point, 18, Pitt St.
ATKENSON Isaac, waggoner, Old Town, beyond Winon St.
ATKINSON Mary, watch maker, South side Second St.
AVESON Richard, hatter, German Lane, between Howard and Liberty Sts.
AYLER Nicholas, potter, Whiskey Alley, between Howard and Eutau Sts. South of Baltimore St.

BAGWELL Thomas, dry and wet goods store, 8, Market st., Fell's Point.
BAHON Stephen, blacksmith, 62, Nor. Gay str.
BAHLER Andrew, house carpenter and joiner, 30, So. How'd str.
BAILEY William, copper smith & tinman, 225, Baltimore St.
BAILEY Thomas, store West India goods, 103, South st. Bowley's wharf
BAILEY & Wilson, copper smiths and tinmen, 12 Cheap-side.
BAILEY Enoch, Coffee House, 38, market place.
---Ditto, grocery and fruit store, 29, Baltimore st.
BAILEY Thomas, dwelling, Old Town, Granby st.
BAILLE John, cooper, Fell's Point, 15, Fells St.
BAIRD William, block maker, 51, Fell's Point, back of Bond st.
BAILER William, cordwainer, Old Town, 92, So. High st.
BAKER William, dry goods store & hardward, 99, Baltimore st.
BAKER Joseph, taylor, 59, Charles st.
BAKER Benjamin, ship carpenter, Fell's Point, 1, Thames st.
BAKER John, innkeeper, do. 13, do.
BAKER Westley, physician, do. 4, George st.
BAKER James, surveyor, Old Town, Jones st.
BAKER Henry, carpenter, Eutau st.
BALL William, gold and silver smith, 62.Baltimore st.
BALL John, residence, 1, Cheapside
BALL Samuel, cutler, Fell's Point, Duke st.
BALABREGA Mary, widow, grocer, 44, So. Calvert st.
BALENTINE Mary, widow, washerwoman, Fell's Point, Strawbury Alley
BALDWIN Richard, hay weigher, Lemmons Alley.
BALDERSTON Isaiah, wire manufacturer and fan maker, Old Town, 31, Front st.
BANK of Discount and Deposit, 48, Baltimore st.
BANK of Maryland, 20, South st.
BANKSON Joseph, 34, South st.
BANGE Jean Jacques, of St. Domingo Waggon Alley

BANTZ John, trunk maker, 23, Second st.
BARCLAY & M'KEAN, merchants, 71, Baltimore st.
BARCLAY Hugh, vendue cryer, Conowago st.
BARRY Standish, clock and watchmaker, 92, Baltimore st.
--- Ditto, dwelling, 20, No. Gay st.
BARRY James, Merchant, 100, Baltimore st.
--- Ditto, dwelling, counting and ware houses, East st.
--- Ditto, Scat, Bank street near Fell's Point.
BARRY Lawrence, drayman, Saratoga st.
BARRY Lovlin, dry goods store, Old Town, 29, Bridge st.
BARRY James, mariner, Eden st.
BARRY John, dwelling, Fish st.
BARNABY Elias, cordwainer, 47, South st.
BARTON Seth, merchant, dwelling and store, 22, South st.
BAROUS & POIRRIER, upholsterers, 61, South st.
BAUSMAN Lawrence & John CURRIERS, 8, Cheapside
BAUSMAN John Currier, dwelling, So. Forrest st.
BAUSMAN Lawrence Currier, dwelling, Fayetts st.
BARGE Andrew, grocer, 24, Cheapside.
BARGE Andrew, dwelling, 50, Pratt st.
BASSETT Isaac, denitst, 25, So. Gay st.
BARNEY Joshua, Sea captain, 19, Commerce st.
BAXTER James, blacksmith, 27, Light st.
BARBARIN Lewis, taylor, 76, Charles st.
BARTALINE Joseph, baker, No. side Camd. st.
BAXLEY John, jun. dwelling, No. Liberty st. West side.
BARCKMAN John, butcher and sausage maker, Fayette st.
BATES Ann, widow, huskster, Waggon Alley.
BAYOTTE Bijotte, widow, of St. Domingo, 13, Liberty st.
BARBER John Francis, Fell's Point, 46 Thames st.
BARKER Joseph, carman Old Town, So. Hight st.
BARROW, merchant, do. Albermarle st.
BARLAND John, taylor, do. do.
BARE Richard, sweep master, Hanover st. Federal Hill
BARNES William, Sea captain, Goodman st. do.
BARNHART Jacob, carpenter, Old Town, Stigers lane.
BARLING Aaron, Innkeeper, Queen st.
BAUHM, Christian, carpenter, Green, No. of Market st.
BARRET Thomas, Ebenist, 42, Harrison st.
BATTY Frederick, taylor, 35, do.
BEDFORD Morton, gold and silversmith, 10, Water st.
BENSON Richard, taylor, 1, South st.
--- Ditto, taylor, dwelling, 100, Hanover st.
BENSON William, house carpenter, East st.
BELLOWS John, & Co. grocers, 6, South st.
BELTON William, merchant taylor, 28, So. Gay st.
BERNARD Lewis Merchant, dwelling, 21, Pratt st.
BUAUDU William, merchant, 24, So. Gay st.
BENTALOU Paul, mercht. dwelling and count. house, 18, So. Gay st.
BESSON Louis, saddler, 52, No. Gay st.
BERTRAND Tousaint, jeweller, 5, No. Gay st.
BETHUNE George, ship chandlers store, 6, Bowley's wharf.
BENOIT Jean Baptiste, gold and silver smith, 29, Charles st.
BENNET John, painter and glazier, 23, So. Howard st.
BENNET Patrick, grocer, Fell's Point, 4, Bond st.

BENNET Patrick, store, do. 14, Fleet st.
--- Ditto dwelling,   do. 16,   do.
BENNET Joseph, Hatter, Welcome Alley, Federal Hill
BENNET William, blacksmith, St. Paul's Lane.
BENNET John, button mould maker, Eutau st.
BEZE Peter, hatter, 31, Charles st.
BECKLEY Henry, house carpenter, 44, Howard st.
BERKMAN Peter, house carpenter, No. side Camd. st.
BENTINE Frederick, shop keeper, 7, Liberty st.
BERTRAND Mary, widow, of St. Domingo, 11, Liberty st.
BERIER Francois Jacques, auditor to Fr. Consul, Cow-pen Lane.
BENZER Peter, wine cooper, Forrest Lane.
BEAMER Frederick, house carpenter, Germ. Lane, between Hd. and East sts.
BESSE Claudius, Sea captain, Fell's Point, 31, Philpot st.
BERNARD John, tavern and boarding house, do. 29, Fell's st.
BELT Walter, Revenue Officer,   do. 17, George st.
BERTRAND Peter, store keeper, dry goods, do. 63, Bond st. back
BEVAN Elizabeth, widow,   do. 95,   do.
BEYZAND William, Sea captain,   do. 16, Philpot st.
BEAMAN James, ship chandler, ·   do. 16, George st.
--- Ditto store,   do. 18,   do.
BERRY James, labourer, No. Forrest st. West side.
BERRY Rajus, tanner, French alley, between Charles and Sharp sts.
BERRY Peter, wood corder, Fell's Point, Ann st.
BERRY Ferdinand, cabinet maker,   do. 88, Bond st.
BERRY Robert,   do.   do. Wolf, corner of Alissanna st.
BERRY Richard, dwelling, Old Town, So. Green st.
BERRY Michael, labourer, Welcome Alley, Fed. Hill.
BEATTY John, labourer,   do.   do.
BENTLEY John, mariner, Old Town, Carolina st.
BEACH Samuel cordwainer,   do. 29, French st.
BEESAW Richard, gardiner,   do. Stigers lane.
BEVANS John, drayman,   do. Eden st.
BERNARD Gabriel, of St. Domingo alley between Light and Charles sts.
BENTER John, carpenter, Pratt st.
BEETLE Richard, labourer, German st.
BECK -----limner, 19, Second st.
BEAMER Elizabeth, widow, boarding house, South side Second st.
BETEL John, mariner, Primrose Alley, between Light and Charles sts.
BENDER Jacob, blacksmith, Boundary st.
BERNARD Peter, clergyman, Boundary st.
BEETLE Henry, taylor, Montgomery st. Federal Hill.
BENFIELD Richard, labourer, Fish st.
BEND --- clergyman, No. West st.
BESON --- 31, Harrison st.
BIGGER Gilbert, watch and clock maker, 115, Baltimore st.
BIER Philip & Co. store keepers, dry goods, 134, Baltimore st.
BIGER Paul, 48, Charles st.
BICKHAM John, tavern keeper, 2, No. Charles st.
BISOIRE --- of St. Domingo, No. Forrest st.
BISHOP Henry, merchant, dwelling 3, Liberty st.
BIAYS James, ship joiner, Fell's Point, 21, Thames st.
--- Ditto, shop,   do. 23,   do.
BIAYS James, ship joiner, shop, do. So. side Queen st.
BIAYS Joseph, ship joiner, do. 23, Fell's st.
BIAYS Joseph, ship joiner, dwelling, do. 16 Shakespears Alley.

BIAYS Joseph, office, do. 26, Fell's st.
BINGLEY John, hair dresser, do. 50, Bond st.
BINGHAM Dianna, washerwoman, do. 30, Fleet st.
BITTERN Lewis, Physician, Old Town, beyond Winon st.
BINNHAM John, drayman, do. do.
BLACK James, school master, 95, Howard st. back
BLACK John, Sharp st.
BLACK Mathew, schoolmaster, room, East st. Between St. Paul's Lane and Charles st.
BLEAKE Mary, Old Town, Carolina st.
BLOOR John, carpenter and joiner, Bank st. near Fell's Point.
BONSALL Robert, store keeper, dry goods, 43, Baltimore st.
BODLEY Thomas, hat manufactory, 178, Baltimore st.
BOSTWICK and MARTIN, grocers, 222, Baltimore st.
BOHN & SLINGLAFF, flour and grocery store, 272, Baltimore st.
BOLTE & YUNK, flour and grocery store, 241, Baltimore st.
BOTNER Elias, Saddle and Harness maker, 7, Cheapside,
BOTNER Elias, dwelling, 28, Water st.
BOISLANDRY Robert Charles, merchant, 29, Water st.
BOWERS John, H. merchant store, & Counting House, 32, McClures wharf.
BOIZEAUX --- of St. Domingo, 32, Charles st.
BOSLEY Joshua, grocer, 1, Market place.
BOULETTE --- Sea captain, 76, Charles st.
BOSE Jacob, dry goods store, 23, No. Howard st.
BOYD Andrew, dwelling, East st. between St. Paul's Lane and Charles st.
BOYD James P. attorney at law. do. do.
BOYD Andrew, brickmaker, Hill st. Federal Hill
BONCHETTS Jacob, painter and glazier, Eutau st.
BOISSARD --- of St. Domingo, Waggon Alley, 70, between Lib. and Eutau sts.
BOYER John, musician, Waggon Alley, West of Howard st.
BOSTON Benjamin, waterman, do. do.
BONLY Jean Jacques, joiner, of St. Domingo, 13, Liberty st.
BOND Richard, schoolmaster, 232, Baltimore st.
--- Ditto, schoolhouse, Dutch Alley, between Howard and Liberty sts.
BOND Richard, carpenter, Old Town, 22, Fridge st.
BOND Peter, hatter, Old Town, 13, Bridge st.
BOND Mordecai, carpenter, do. North st.
BOND John, carpenter, do. So. Green st.
BOOK George, constable, Fell's Point, 93, back of Pond st.
BOYER John, house carpenter, Fell's Point, 21, Market st.
BONFIELD John, ship carpenter, do. 13, Skakespears Alley.
BOND Hannah, washerwoman, do. Strawbury Alley, between Wilks and Alisanna sts.
BOUILLIETTS & FOLIER, boarding house, do, 30, Philpot st.
BOLINS Henry, carpenter, do. 12, Alissanna st.
BOWERS Conrad, butcher, So. Howard st.
BOWERS John, comb maker, do. beyond Winon st.
BOWERS William inn keeper, do. do.
BOWERS George, bricklayer, do. do.
BOWERS Martin, wet and dry goods store, do. do.
BORIN John, carman, do. do.
BOWEN Labrett, carpenter, do. 26, So. High st.
BOISSON John, do. Albermarle st.
BOYER John, iron and nail manufactory, do. Granby st.
BONNE Madam, Fell's Point, 10, Wilks st.
BOYD James, cordwainer, Old Town, So. Green st.
BOGGIT Michael, labourer, do. Wapping st.

BOYCE Thomas, carman, Parre st. Federal Hill.
BODMUN John, stage driver, Whiskey Alley, between Howard and Eutau sts. So. of Baltimore st.
BOTTS John, carpenter,   do.   do.
BOOTH Abraham, drayman, passage back of St. Paul's Lane.
BOWSER Richard, mariner, So. Frederick st.
BRICE John, wet and dry goods store, 9, Baltimore st.
BROWN George, physician, 28, Baltimore st.
BROWN Henry, tobacconist, 164, Baltimore st.
BROWN Aquila, merchant, dwelling, 274, Baltimore st.
--- Ditto, merchant, counting house, 16, Water st.
BROWN William, currier, 15, Water st.
BROWN James, house carpenter, 27, No. Gay st.
BROWN Joshua, Huckster, 21, Light st.
BROWN Jacob, taylor, 7, County Wharf.
BROWN Thomas horse doctor, East between Calvert and Gay st.
BROWN Justice, Printer, East between St. Paul's Lane & Charles sts.
BROWN Henry, drayman, Waggon Alley, West of Howard st.
BROWN Benjamin, labourer, Forrest Lane.
BROWN Dickson, ship carpenter, Fell's Point, 19, Philpot st.
BROWN James, labourer,   do. West side Bond st. upper end.
BROWN John, mariner, do. Fleet between Bond and Market sts.
BROWN London, ship scraper, do. Happy Alley
BROWN James, labourer, do. Wueen st.
BROWN Charles, mariner, do. 86, Bond st.
BROWN Benjamin, ship carpenter, do. Alisanna st.
BROWN John, potter, Old Town, 22, Bridge st.
BROWN William, cabinet maker, do. So. High st.
--- Ditto dwelling   do. Albermarle st.
BROWN Jesse, taylor, do. Albermarle st.
BROWN David David, do. Granby st.
BROWN Josiah, dry goods store, Fell's Point, 10, Market st.
BROWN James, boatman, So. Frederic st.
BROWN Alexander, cabinet maker, Harrison st.
BRANSON William, hatter, 131, Baltimore st.
BRANSON Michael, brass founder, 148, Baltimore st.
BRIEN Susannah, huckster, 25, South st.
BRIEN Daniel, Fell's Point, 4, Queen st.
BRIEN John, carpenter, Front st. West from Calvert st.
BRYAN Jacob, labourer, Waggon Alley, East of Howard st.
BRYAN Abraham, do.   do.   do.
BROTHERTON Thomas, cordwainer, 22, No. Gay st.
BROTHERS Henry, 71, Howard st.
BRYDAN James, Fountain Inn, 3, Light st.
BRYER Emanuel, 78, Charles st.
BRADISH John, grocer, 9, Pratt st.
BRINDEL Frederick, bricklayer, 46, No. Howard st.
BRESSON --- of St. Domingo, dwelling, Fayette between Howard and Eutau sts.
BREDENODER Adam, baker, Fell's Point, ?9, Bond st.
BREMON John, tinman,   do. 65, back of Bond st.
BRIGNOLE Peter, Sea captain, do. 45, Market st.
BRALY Silvester, street paver, Fell's Point, Happy Alley.
BRYSON James, carman, Old Town, beyond Winon st.
BRYSON John, stone cutter, do. No. Winon st.
BRITTAIN John, drayman, do. Temple st.

BRADY John, labourer,   do. Duke st.
BROOKMAN Jane, widow, Fell's Point, 11, Wilks st.
BRUNER Andrew, sugar baker, Forrest st. Federal Hill.
BREIDENBURGH Valentine, plaisterer, Old Town, 27, French st.
BREIDENBURGH John, tallow chandler, Fish st.
BRISSAU Francis, carpenter, Eden st.
BRISTER Samuel, labourer, Barre st. Federal Hill
BRAHAN Sarah, seamstress, Sharp st.
BREVITT John, grocer, East, between St. Paul's Lane and Charles st.
BUCHANAN and SAVAGE, shoe manufactory, 48, Baltimore st.
BUCHANAN & COLE, physicians, 196, Baltimore st.
BUCHANAN & YOUNG, merchants, 135, Baltimore st.
BUCHANAN, SPEAR & Co., hard ware store, 8, No. Gay st.
BUCHANAN William, dwelling 44, So. Gay st.
BUCHANAN James, dwelling, 9, Charles st.
BUCHANAN Andrew, merchant, dwelling, 200, Baltimore st.
BUCHANAN, Andrew and Loyd, merchants, store, 13, So. Calvert st.
--- Ditto, ware house, Lovely Lane, between Calvert and South sts.
BURNESTON Isaac, dry goods store, 99, Baltimore st.
BURNESTON Isaac, merchant, dwelling, East between Calvert and Gay sts.
BURNESTON Joseph, hatter, Fell's Point, 17, George st.
--- Ditto, shop,   do. 19,   do.
BUCKLER William, dry goods store, 133, Baltimore st.
BUCKLER William, merchant, dwelling, 2, St. Paul's Lane.
BUFFY Thomas, D. gold and silver smith, 140, Baltimore st.
BUCKINGHAM Thomas, flour inspector, 72, Hanover st.
BURN John, house carpenter and joiner, South side Camd. st.
BURNS John, waggoner, Saratoga st.
BUTTLER Anthony, gentleman's servant, North st.
BUTTLER Joanna, washerwoman,   do.
BUTTLER Nancy, widow, Primrose Alley, between Light and Charles sts.
BURGOIGNE Andrew Louis, Sea captain, Fell's Point, Wills between Philpot
and Queen sts.
BURROWS Thomas, painter and glazier, do. 3, Fell's st.
BURNSIDE James, cordwainer, do. 7,   do.
BUNKER Samuel, Sea captain, do. 123, Bond st. back
BUNKER Job, Sea captain, do. East side Bond st. upper end.
BUSS John, waterman, Fell's Point, Apple Alley, between Shakespear's Alley
and Fleet st.
BURCK Thomas, mariner, do. do. between Alisa-na and Fleet sts.
BURCKE schoolmaster, do. 9, Fleet between Bond and Market sts.
BURSURD Richard, cordwainer, do. Alisanna st.
BUNTZ Jacob, ship carpenter, do. Ann between Pitt & Alisanna sts.
BURKE David, dry goods store, do. 2, Philpot st.
BURKE David, boat builder, do. 22, do.
BURKE Massey, grocer, do. Alisanna st.
BURKE John, miller, Old Town, So. Green st.
--- Ditto, dwelling, do. 53, Bridge st.
BURKE William, do. do. do. 53, do.
BURKE Richard, drayman, 36, Wilks st.
BURKE Miles, journeyman coachmaker, at Nathan Garvin's Second st.
BURKE Charles, waitingman, So. Federick st.
BUTTON Elias, stevedore, Fell's Point, 38, Thames st.
BUTTON Robert, constable, Old Town, Forrest st.
BUTTON George, tinman, Eden st.

BUCK Thomas, sawyer, Old Town, So. Winon st.
BUCK John. butcher, Carolina st.
BUCKLEY Lawrence, cordwainer, 15, Wilks st.
BULL James, cordwainer, Triplets Alley.
BULL William, clark, So. Frederick st.
BULLEN Simon, cordwainer, 69, Harrison st.
BUDD Elizabeth, widow, Public Alley.
BUDDLER John, Inn-keeper, Front, West from Calvert st.
BRYAN Joseph, carman, Fell's Point, between Alisanna & Fleet sts.
BYRNE James, Revenue Officer, do. 30, Pitt st.

CALMAN & Co. grocers, 10, Baltimore St.
--- Ditto, dry goods store, 12, do.
CASEY Robert, skin dresser and leather breeches maker, 30, Baltimore st.
CARRUTHERS I. & D., merchants, 125, Baltimoer St.
CARRICK Arthur, druggist and apothecary, 29, So. Calvert St.
CAUSTEN Isaac, grocer, 39, South st.
CASENAVE & WALKER, merchants 21, Water St.
CAMPBELL Archibald, dwelling, 14 So. Gay St.
--- Ditto, counting house, 16, do.
--- Ditto, ware house, 53, So. Gay St.
CAMBELL George, tobacco spinner, Fell's Point, 61, Bond st.
CALWELL Thomas, dwelling, Old Town, 21, So. High st.
CAMPARIO John, shop keeper, 66, Charles st.
CALL Catherine, widow, sausage maker, South side Lexington st.
CABERIRO John, segar maker, 4, No. Frederick st.
CANTWELL Thomas, flour and grocery store, 39, No. Howard st.
CANNON Ann, widow, washerwoman, Olt Town, 31, French st.
CATON Richard, merchant, dwelling, Old Town, Ploughman st.
CAPPEAU --- of St. Domingo, Carolina st.
CAPIDO George, baker, Federal Hill, Brioy Alley
CAREY James, flour store, 47, Light st.
CAREY Dennis, Inn keeper, Fell's Point, 6, Thames st.
CAREY John, labourer, do. 40, Wilks st.
CARTER David, grocer, 3, County wharf.
CARTER Solomon, 3, do.
CARTER Jane, huckster, Fell's Point, 44, Thames st.
CARTER Robert, dwelling, Old Town, So. Green st.
CARTER Francis, upholsterer, Alley, between Light and Charles sts.
CARR Joseph, Music store, 6, No. Gay st.
CARR Thomas, brewer, dwelling, 19, Pratt st.
CARR Peter, cordwainer, Fell's Point, 51, Bond st.
CARLISLE Ann, widow, seamstress, Carolina st.
CARMICHAEL Deagle, drayman, Conowago st.
CARMAN Patrick,labourer, German lane, between Howard and Eutau sts.
CARMAN William, carpenter, Old Town, 77, So. High st.
CARWAY George, carman, Eutau, So. of Baltimore st.
CARNAGHAN George, carpenter, King George st.
CATOR and BROTHERS, grocers, 9, County wharf.
CAPLES William, drayman, Waggon Alley, West of Baltimore st.
CARPENTER William, schoolmaster, Old Town, York st.
CARROL Mary, seamstress, French Alley, between Charles and Sharp sts.
CARROL Mary Ann, schoolmistress, Ruston Lane, between Light and Charles sts.
CARROL John, Bishop, No. West st. adjoining the Roman Church.
CARRERE John, merchant, dwelling and couting house, 8, Harrison st.
CARSON William, grocer, Fell's Point, Lancaster Alley

CARSON Andrew, grocer, Old Town, York st.
CASEY Robert, coach painter, shop, So. Frederic st.
CASSIDY Hannah, widow, 21, No. Frederic st.
CASSAYEAU Bernard, of St. Domingo, Old Town, North st.
CASTAING Benoit, of St. Domingo, Old Town Jones st.
CASSEDY ---, shop keeper, Fell's Point, 55, Bond st.
CASWELL Josiah & FUNK, Inn-keepers 73, No. Howard st.
CEBRON Olivier, shop keeper, 29, Light st.
CHAMBERS Francis, hair-dresser and perfumer, 67, Baltimore st.
CHAMBERS Thomas, waterman, Fell's Point, Alisanna st.
CHAMBERS William, potter, Old Town, So. Green st.
CHADICK Sarah, widow, Old Town, No. Winon st.
CHADICK Frances, mantua maker, No. Winon st.
CHALMERS John, ship chandler's store, 1, Cheapside.
--- Ditto, rope store, Fell's Point, 26, Fell's st.
CHALMERS James, shop keeper, 53, No. Howard st.
CHAMPAYNE J. R. merchant, dwelling, 42, South st.
CHAMPAYNE & DEYME, counting house, 26, Commerce st.
CHANCONIE --- of St. Domingo, No. Liberty st.
CHAMILLON Joseph, Inn-keeper, Fell's Point, 29, Thames st.
CHANDLER James, ship carpenter, 82, Charles st.
CHANGEURS sons, of Peter & Co, merchants, So. Gay st.
CHATTEL Mary, widow, Old Town, Pitt st.
CHATTERTON Azunbush, widow, millener, Fell's Point, 27, George st
CHAPEAU Anthony, Fell's Point, 83, Bond st.
CHAPMAN Nuthill, brass founder, 52, No. Frederic st.
CHASE Samuel, Judge of Supreme Court of Maryland, corner of Lexington and
Eutau sts.
CHASE H., physician, Old Town, 22, Bridge st.
CHAUSSE Etienne, 86, Hanover st.
CHEDAL Francois, tinman, 32, Baltimore st.
CHEVALIER John Abraham, sculptor, 18, St. Paul's Lane.
CHEVALIER --- dwelling, 66, South st.
CHESTER Samuel, recruiting officer, Conowago st.
CHESNUT James Inn-keeper, Fell's Point, 13, Wilks st.
CHINNUTH Arthur, grain and flour store, Old Town, 26, Bridge st.
CHURCHMAN Enoch, dwelling 57, No. Gay st.
CHRISTY Eleaner, widow, 106, Hanover st.
CICERON Anthony, hair-dresser, Fell's Point, 28, Bond st.
CLARKE Ambrose, 141, Baltimore st.
CLARK Joseph, Inn-keeper, Fell's Point, 3, Pitt st.
CLARK John, Sea captain, Fell's Point, 25, Pitt st.
CLARKE Oliver, mariner, Fell's Point, Apple Alley, between Alissanna and
Fleet sts.
CLARKE Joshua, hatter, Fell's Point, Apple Alley, between Alisanna and Fleet
sts.
CLARKE Matthew, mariner, Fell's Point, 94, Bond st.
CLARKE John, wheelwright, Old Town, beyond Winon st.
CLARKE Jacob, drayman, Old Town, So. Green st.
CLARKE John, bricklayer, Old Town, 18, So. High st.
CLARKE Joseph, architect, Old Town, 21, So. High st.
CLARK Ann, widow, Old Town, 41, French st.
CLARKE Richard, labourer, Welcome Alley, Federal Hill.
CLARKE Joseph, labourer, back of East st.
CLARKE Joseph, cordwainer, Old Town, 20, French st.
CLAYLAND Dobbin & Co., Printers of the Baltimore Telegraphe, 36, Baltimore st.

CLAGETT H. & J. grocers, 215, Baltimore st.
CLAPHAM Jonas, merchant, Old Town, 65, Front st.
CLACKNER Adam, bricklayer, King George st.
CLAYTON Richard, cordwainer, Ruxton Lane, between Light and Charles sts.
CLAUS Stephen, Inn-keeper, Fell's Point, 92, Bond st.
CLEBBORN George, Sea Captain, Old Town, 12, Phipot st.
CLELAND Samuel, Fell's Point, 12, George st.
CLEMENTS Josias, dry good store, 36, Baltimore st.
CLEM William, copper store, 128, Baltimore st.
CLARKE James, cordwainer, 39, Fell's Point, Bond st.
CLINE Peggy and Mary, seamstress, So. Liberty st.
CLINE Casper, stage driver, Barre st. Federal Hill.
CLINES Elizabeth, widow, Paca st.
CLINGAN and SIMPSON, merchants. store & counting house, 85, South st. Bowleys
wharf.
CLOEHARTY Patrick, shop keeper, 115, Howard st.
CLOPPER John, baker, 9, Light st.
CLOPPER Cornelius, dwelling, 55, Charles st.
CLOPPER Peter, sail maker, Fell's Piont, Petty coat Lane
CLOPDORE Philip, butcher, Brioy ailey, Federal Hill.
CLOSE Christian, grain store, 29, No. Howard st.
CLUNEY James, Tavern and boarding house, 25, Fell's Point
CLYMER Catherine, widow, Old Town, Forrest st.
COAD David, Tavern & Boarding house, Fell's Point, 17, Bond st.
COATES Jonathan, schoolmaster, dwelling, 60, No. Fredrick st.
--- Ditto school room, Triplets alley.
COATES Francis, baker, Public alley.
COBAULT Ludwic, Journeyman apothecary, Cyder alley
COCHRAM Mecker & Co., merchants, 12, South st.
COCHRAN Hiram, sail maker, loft, 13, County wharf.
--- Ditto dwelling,   17, Pratt st.
COCKEY Joshua, labourer, 50, No. Gay st.
COFFEY Susannah, widow, schoolmistress, East, between St. Pauls Lane and No.
Charles st.
COLDWELL john, wheelright, Old Town, North st.
COLE & Compy, dry good store, 81, Baltimore st.
COLE Charles, taylor & habit maker, shop, 211, Baltimore st.
COLE Charles, dwelling,   7, Liberty st.
COLE William, merchant, 4, South St.
COLE Sarah, widow, midwife, Waggon alley, West of Howard st.
COLE Joshua, carpenter, Waggon alley, East of Howard st.
COLE Margaret, widow, boarding house, Fell's Point, 23, George st.
COLE Frederic, huckster, Old Town, 96, So. High St.
COLE Jacob, windsor chair maker, Old Town, 73, Front St.
COLE Godfrey,   Old Town, 85, So. High St.
COLE & Brothers, chair makers, Old Town, 89, So. High St.
COLE John, carpenter, Old Town, Pitt St.
COLHOUN James, merchant, 90, Baltimore St.
COLER John, Blacksmith, 36, Light St.
COLEMAN Joseph, ship joiner, Fell's Point, 35, Philpots St.
COLEMAN William, ship joiner, Fell's Point, Strawbury alley.
COLVIN Richard, store keeper, Old Town, 16, Bridge St.
COLVIN Daniel, physician, Old Town, corner of Wapping St.
COLLINS William, plaisterer, 84, Hanover St.
COLLINS Henry, ship carpenter, Fell's Point, Alisanna St.

COLLINS Hugh, labourer, Old Town, Stigers Lane.
COLLUMBET Rene, Old Town, 23, Front St.
COMEGYS Benjamin & Co. merchants, 85, Baltimore St.
COMMER Margaret, widow, seamstress, 14, So. Howard st.
COMPTE Julian, of St. Domingo, 23, Pratt st.
CONAWAY William, ship carpenter, No. side Camdon st.
CONWAY John, cooper, Fell's Point, 34, Queen st.
CONWAY Robert, carpenter, Fell's Point, 100, Bond st.
CONWAY James, saddler, Old Town, 55, So. High st.
CONOVER William, coach maker, Sharp st.
COPELAND Robert, watch maker, Fell's Point, 9, Thames st.
CONCKLIN John, blacksmith, Fell's Point, 21, Shakespears Alley
CONSTABLE Thomas, carpenter & joiner, Old Town, Jones st.
CONSTABLE Charles, carpenter & joiner, Old Town, Jones st.
CONSTABLE John, carpenter, Old Town, 24, Franch st.
CONSTANTINE Richard, stage driver 75, Hanover st.
CORBETT William, baker, Waggon Alley, West of Howard st.
CORNTHWAIT Robert, bran & meal store, Fell's Point 98, Bond st.
CORRIE James, grocery store, 26, Cheapside.
COSKERY Bernard, nail maker, 105., No. Howard st.
COULIER Alexander, saddle & harness maker, 116, Baltimore st.
COULTER John, physician, dwelling, Fell's Point, 27, Alisanna st.
--- Ditto   druggist shop, Fell's Point, 29, Alisana st.
COULSON Patty, widow, Old Town, Albermarle st.
COUTIER Jean Baptiste, pastry cook, 64, Charles st.
COURTENEY Robert, merchant, 97, Baltimore st.
COURTENAY Hercules, secretary of Maryland insurance company, 16, South st.
COURTENAY Montgomery, widow, seamstress, German Lane, between Hanover &
Howard sts.
COURTNAY James, cooper, Old Town, Albermarle st.
COWARD Richard, sea captain, Fell's Point, 37, Philpot st.
COX Mathew, ship carpenter, Fell's Point, 7, Pitt st.
COX Cussy, labourer, passage back of St. Pauls Lane.
CONNELLY Patrick, drayman, Waggon Alley, West of Howard st.
CONNOLY Michael, labourer, Old Town, Albermarle st.
CONNOR ---, Pilot, Fell's Point, Alisanna st.
CONNOR ---, widow, washerwoman, Old Town, 15, Bridge st.
COULLING James, taylor, 18, Charles st.
COURRAGE James, of St. Domingo, Waggon Alley, West of Howard st.
COOK John, shop keeper, 52, No. Howard st.
COOK Henry, stage driver, 21, South st.
COOKE William, dry good store, Fell's Point, 11 Bond st.
COOK James, labourer, Old Town, Bridge, beyond Winon st.
COOK Margaret, washerwoman,
COOK John, labourer, Eutau st.
COOMBS John, labourer, Fell's Point, Strawberry Alley.
COOPER John, labourer, Saratoga st.
COOPER Thomas, Sea captain, Fell's Point, 24, Fleet st.
COOPER Agnes, widow, seamstress, Fell's Point, 13, Wilks st.
COOPER Jacob, labourer, Old Town, French st. Precincts.
COOPER Thomas, drayman,
CRAIG Collins, mariner, Ruxton Lane, between Charles and Light sts.
CRAIN Thomas, carpenter, Lombard st.
CRANAWAY Solomon, mariner, Goodman st. Federal Hill.
CRANFORD Samuel, cordwainer, Second str. between Gay str. and the Falls.

CRANGLE James, scowman, Welcome Alley, Federal Hill.
CRANCKLE Henry, carman, Old Town, Pitt st.
CRAWFORD Richard, mariner, Fell's Point, West side Bond str.upper end.
CREMER Edward, locksmith, Fell's Point, 92, Bond st.
CREUZBOURG Simon, Whiskey Alley, between How'd & Eutau, So. of Baltimore sts.
CRIPS Jacob, butcher, Carolina st. near Fell's Point.
CROMER Daniel, cooper, Eutau st.
CROMEL Samuel, tanner, German st. between Eutau & Pace sts.
CROMFORD Priscilla, seamstress, Fell's Point, 34, Wilks st.
CROSBY Hannah, widow, boarding house, 1, commerce st.
CROSS Joshua, labourer, Old Town, Bridge st. beyond Winon st.
CROSS Robert, carpenter, So. Frederic st.
CROUCH William, carpenter, King George st.
CROW William, boarding house & tavern, Fell's Point, 9, Bond st.
CROWNMILLER Thomas, blacksmith, So. side Camdon st.
CROXALL James, dwelling, 64, Hanover str.
CRUSE Jacob, currier, dwelling, 83, Hanover st.
--- Ditto   curriers shop, 37, So. Calvert st.
CROOK Walter, cabinet maker, 16, So. Howard st.
CROOK George, butcher, 46, Market Place st.
CULVERWELL Richard, constable, 9, Second st.
CUMMINGS William, umbrella & Oil cloth maker, Old Town, So. Green st.
CUMMINS Mary, Inn keeper, Old Town, Bridge st. beyond winon st.
CUNNINGHAM James, carpenter, Waggon Alley, East of How'd st.
CUNNINGHAM Thomas, sea captain, Fell's Point, 3, Shakespears Alley.
CUNNINGHAM John, sea captain, Fell's Point, 28, Queen st.
CURSON Richard, merchant, dwelling, 20, Light st.
--- Ditto   counting house, 51, Water st.
CURTAIN James, butcher, Fell's Point, Ann, between Pitt and Alisanna sts.
CURTIS Francis, attorney at law, No. side Camdon st.
CURTIS Eleazer, Inn keeper, Fell's Point, 3, Philpot st.
CURTIS Benjamin, Pilot, Fell's Point, Apple Alley, between Alisanna & Fleet sts.
CURTIS John, mariner, Fell's Point, 40, Thames st.
CUSTOM HOUSE OFFICE, 37 So. Gay st.
CUTCHEL Casper, butcher, Saratoga st.

DALRYMPLE John, carpenter, Old Town, 61, South High st.
DANCER William, cordwainer, 1, No. Calvert st.
DANIEL Anthony, sea captain, Fell's Point, 24, Thomas st.
DARCY Michael, Inn keeper, Fell's Point, 1, Alisanna st.
DARDENTIS Marie, Old Town, 16, So. High st.
DASHIELL Richard, ship joiner, Fell's Point, 5, Philpot st.
DASHIELL Benjamin,   Fell's Point, 4, Philpot st.
DASHIELL Charles, ship carpenter, Fell's Point, 12, Shakespears Alley.
DAUGHADY Abraham, blacksmith, Old Town, Bridge st. beyond Winon st.
DAUGHERTY John, dry good store, Old Town, 13, Bridge st.
DAVANNE John, jeweller & gold smith, 80, Baltimore st.
DAVENPORT Jonathan, gold & silver smith, 102, Baltimore st.
DAVENPORT John, dwelling, 11, Pratt st.
DAVIDSON Robert, turner, Old Town, Wapping st.
DAVIDSON Robert, bricklayer, Barre st. Federal Hill.
DAVIDSON James, cabinet maker, 1, Baltimore st.
DAVID Jean, of St. Domingo, 23, Commerce st.
DAVISON William, ship joiner, Fell's Point, 14, Queen st.
DAVIES Fulton, merchant, 159, Baltimore st.
DAVIES Mary, crockery store, Old Town, 18, Bridge st.

DAVIES Samuel, saddler, Old Town, Bridge st. beyond Winon st.
--- Ditto   shop,   Old Town, 51, Bridge st.
DAVIS William, Inn keeper, Fell's Point, 9, George st.
DAVIS John, mariner, Fell's Point, 49, Market st.
DAVIS Peter, sea captain, Fell's Point, Happy Alley.
DAVIS Joseph, boat builder, Fell's Point, 24, Queen st.
DAVIS Thomas, Butcher, Bank st. near Fell's Point.
DAVIS Job, cooper, upper Water st. between Calvert and Light sts.
DAVIS Joseph, grocer, Public Alley.
DAVIS Edward, Inn keeper, Fell's Point, 4, Market st.
DAVY Alex. William, exchange & land broker, 28, office South st.
DAVY William, bricklayer, King George st.
DAVY Henry, cabinet maker, King George st.
DAWES Francis, dwelling, Old Town, So. High st.
--- Ditto dry & wet goods store, Old Town, 35, Bridge st.
DAWES David, carpenter, Old Town, Albermarle st.
DAWSON William, waterman, Fell's Point, 69, Bond st.
DAWSON William, ship joiner, Fell's Point, 26, George st.
DAY John, cordwainer, Old Town, Stigers Lane.
DAY James, barber, 5, No. Frederic st.
DEADY Daniel, shop keeper, 54, No. Howard st.
DEAL Charles, waggoner, Dutch Alley, between Howard and Eutau sts.
DEAL ---, mariner, Fell's Point, Apple Alley.
DEAGLE Simon, sea captain, 55, Charles st.
DEAN Hannah, widow, 5, Second st.
DEAN James, hair dresser, Fell's Point, 9, Thames st.
DEAVER & COULLING, dry good store, 27, Baltimore st.
DEAVER John, dry good store, 185, Baltimore st.
DE BLOKE Francis, broker 24, South st.
DECKER Frederic, dwelling, 28, No. Howard st.
DE CARNAP Jasper, dwelling, 75, Pratt st.
DE CURSE Rogrigue, inspector of the fort, Alley between Light and Charles sts.
DE GLANDE Jean, mariner, 52, Charles st.
DELANY Daniel, counseller at law, 6, St. Pauls Lane
DELANY Peter, weaver & sexton, Cyder Alley, between Eutau and Paca sts.
DELCHER Christian, labourer, Old Town, 45, French st.
DELCHER Valentine, miller, Old Town, French st. Precincts.
DELINO ---   Boundery st.
DELISLE William, grocery store, 12, Pratt st.
DELISLE John, physician, Primrose Alley, between Light and Charles sts.
DELMAS ---, merchant, 23, Light St.
DELMAS Jean Joseph, baker, Fayette st. between Liberty and Howard sts.
DELORY John, labourer, Old Town, Temple st.
DELOZIER Daniel surveyer for the port of Baltimore, dwelling, 26, Water st.
DELUCE Francis, cordwainer, dwelling, Old Town, Granby st.
--- Ditto   shop   70, Baltimore st.
DEMSEY John, labourer, Old Town, Bridge str. beyond Winon st.
DENMEAD Edward, carpenter, 44, No. Liberty st.
DENT & NORRIS, grocery stroe, 21, Cheapside.
DENT George, merchant, dwelling, 17, Bank st.
DENTON James, labourer, Bank st. near Fell's Point.
DENIS John Peter, boarding house, 21, St. Pauls Lane.
DENIS Benjamin, dwelling, 118, No. Howard st.
--- Ditto   grocery store, 59, No. Howard st.
DENNIS Elizabeth, ---Fell's Point, 20, Fell's st.

DENNIS Philip, cordwainer, Old Town, Stigers Lane.
DENUX & VIGNER, wet & dry good store, 7, Baltimore st.
DE RUQUIERE, widow, of St. Domingo, No. side of Camdon st.
DE RUTEZ, --widow of St. Domingo, Fell's Point, Strawberry Alley.
DERASSINE --- , 36, No. Frederic st.
DERRICK Susannah, widow, boarding house, Fell's Point, 12, George street.
DES CHAMPS Peter, labourer,   Alley between Light and Charles sts.
DESK Michael, sugar baker, Montgomery St. Federal Hill.
DESHIELD Louis, Pilot, --- 39, Hanover st.
DESPORT Joseph, ship carpenter, Fell's Point, Queen St.
DESUI James, baker, 24, Harrison St.
DETTMAR Christopher, taylor, So. Frederic St.
DE VALCOURT Alexander, merchant, 40, Charles St.
DEW Robert, taylor, 44, Baltimore St.
DEWITT Thomas, Inn keeper, 14, Market place St.
DEXTER James, waterman, 18, Pratt St.
DEYME John, merchant, dwelling, Commerce St.
DEEGAN Patrick, taylor, 46, So. Charles St.
DEEMS Frederic, hatter, Cow-pen Lane
DICK Williams, schoolmaster, New Church street.
DICK David, cordwainer, 16, No. Frederick street.
DICKSON John, Thomas & William, hardware store, 82, Baltimore street.
DICKSON John, rigger, Fell's Point, Apple Alley.
DICKSON Elizabeth, widow, boarding house, Old Town, Front st.
DICKINSON Edward, ship carpenter, Fell's Point, Wolf street.
DICKINSON Brittingham, ---- Fell's Point, 6, Philpot street.
DIDIER Henry, merchant, 202, Baltimore street.
DIFFENDERFFER Michael, dry & wet good store, 5, Baltimore street.
   Ditto --------- store,   3, Market Place st.
DIFFENDERFFER Peter, hardware store, 23, Baltimore street.
DIFFENDERFFER Daniel, dwelling, Old Town, York street.
DIGEAUX -----------, sea captain, Fell's Point, 82, Bond street.
DILAR Jacob, butcher, Old Town, York street.
DILWORTH William, cooper, dwelling, 9, Second street.
DILWORTH William, junr. cooper, 33, Light st.
DILLON John, scowman, Public Alley.
DIMLO Joseph, innkeeper, Fell's Point, 73, Bond st.
DINSMORE Thomas, flour merchant, 5 North Howard st.
DINSMORE David, huckster, 6, South High st.
DISBY John, inkeeper, Fell's Point, 33, Wilk's st.
DISTRICT COURT OF MARYLAND, Clerks Office of, 10, Nor. Calv. st.
DITERLY Peter, carpenter, Lombard st.
DIXON John, dry good store, 27, So. Calvert st.
DYER Margaret, widow, seamstress, Eutau st.
DYER Fennella, widow, seamstress, 25, St. Paul's Lane.
DYKES William, grocery store, 221, BAltimore st.
DYKES William, grocer, Old Town, Nor. Winon st.
DODGE Samuel, revenue officer, Fell's Point, Pitt street.
DODD John, taylor, dwelling, Old Town, 52, Bridge street.
DONALDSON Joseph, dry good store, 123 Baltimore street
DONALDSON Thomas, notary public, 36, So. GRy street.
DONALON Nehemiah, town collector, 36, So. Gay street.
DONALSON James, sea captain, Goodman street, Federal Hill.
DONALLAN Thomas, gauger for the port of Baltimore, 12, Commerce street.
DONALLY Thomas, flour merchant, 49, No. Howard street.

DONALLY James, drayman, Old Town, So. Green street.
DONALLY Hugh, bricklayer, French Alley, between Charles and Sharp streets.
DONNELLY Daniel, schoolmaster, Fell's Point, 46, Bond street.
DONOVAN Bartholemy, Inn keeper, 36, Water street.
DONOVAN Thomas, Inn keeper, Old Town, 15, So. High street.
DONOVAN Valentine, carpenter, Old Town, So. Green street.
DONNOLY James, bricklayer, Brioy Alley, Federal Hill.
DOODLE James, labourer, Barre street, Federal Hill.
DORMAN William, mariner, Fell's Point, 4, Shakespears Alley.
DORSEY Walter, attorney and councellor at law, 198, Baltimore st.
DORSEY John E., anchor and nail store, 1, County Wharf.
DORSEY Priscilla, washerwoman, Forrest Lane.
DORSEY Philip, mathematical instrument maker, Fell's Point, 20, Queen street.
--- Ditto, dwelling, Fell's Point, 62, Thames street.
DORSEY Edward, Sawyer, Old Town, Forrest street.
DORSEY James, carpenter, 71, Water street.
DOUGHDAY Abraham, blacksmith, Old Town, North street.
DOUGHERTY John, cabinet maker, 148, Baltimore street, back.
DOUGHERTY John, dry good store, Old Town, 13, Bridge street.
DOUGLAS John, mariner, Fell's Point, Nor. side Lancaster Alley.
DOUGLAS William, taylor, Fell's Point, Ann street, between Pitt and Alisanna
streets.
DOUGLASS George, Cordwainer, 60, No. Frederic street.
DOUGLASS Philip, oysterman, Old Town, Bridge street, beyond winon street.
DOWLING John, mariner, Honey Alley, Federal Hill.
DOWSE Primus, labourer, North street, Log Town
DOYLE James, labourer, Hill street, Federal Hill.
DOYLE George, Inn keeper, Eutau street, corner of Dutch Alley.
DOYNE John, dry good store, 2, Baltimore street.
DRAVES Mary, widow, huckster, Second street, between Gay st. and the Falls.
DRAWBACK John, cooper, So. Frederic street.
DREBERT Andrew, tinman, 74, Hanover street.
DREBERT Christian, blacksmith, 86, Charles street.
DROHDNIER George, clergyman, 11, Second street.
DROUILLARD Andrew, of St. Domingo, Fell's Point, Fleet street.
DROWN Thomas, taylor and grocer, Old Town, Bridge street between Winon street.
DU BUC Peter, cooper, Bank street, near Fell's Point.
DUBLIN Thomas, carpenter, Primrose Alley, between Light and Charles streets.
DUCATEL Edmen(?), druggist and chemist, 26, Baltimore street.
DUCHMIN Francois, --- German street, between Liberty and Howard streets.
DUCLOS ---, French cook, Upper Water street.
DUDLEY Edward, watchman, North street, Log Town.
DUDLEY James, ship carpenter, Fell's Point, Argyle Alley.
DUFFEY Owen, bricklayer, Old Town, So. High street.
DUGAN Patrick, taylor, 38, So. Calvert street.
DUGAN Cumberland, dwelling, 26, So. Gay street.
--- Ditto. ----- rope store, 66, Water street.
DUKEHART Henry, grocery store, 13, Baltimore street.
--- Ditto. ----- bakers shop, 15, Baltimore street.
DUMAS Thomas, sea captain, Fell's Point, 13, Alisanna street.
DUMOUCHEL Francis Charles, of Guadaloupe, Fell's Point, west side Bond street,
upper end.
DUNAVON Timothy, labourer, Welcome Alley, Federal Hill.
DUNAVON Samuel, fruiterer, Second street, So. side.
DUNCAN William, coopers shop, 49, So. Gay street.

DUNCAN James, sea captain, Fell's Point, North side Fleet st.
DUNCAN Thomas, carpenter, Fell's Point, Apple Alley.
DUNCAN William, sea captain, Triplets Alley.
DUNGAN Esther, huckster, 74, No. Howard st.
DUNONGVALL --- , of St. Domingo, 88, No. Howard st.
DUPEROU --- , of St. Domingo, 2, No. Frederic st.
DUROCHE Mary, widow, of St. Domingo, Fayette st. between Liberty and Howard
sts.
DUTOYAS John, taylor, Fell's Point, 37, Bond st.
DUTRO George, taylor, North st. Log Town.
DWYER & ROBERTS, grocers, Fell's Point, 2, Market st.

EAGLESTON Abraham, carpenter, Bank st. near Fell's Point.
EARL & HUMPHREYVILLE, flour merchants, 33, No. Howard st.
EARMAN John, chair maker French Alley, between Charles and Sharp sts.
EARNEST George, cordwainer, Front st. West of Calvert st.
EASTON Eliza, widow, tavern and boarding house, 59, South st.
EATON Sarah, tayloress, Fell's Point, Alisanna st.
EBERT Martin, weaver, Whiskey Alley, between Howard and Eutau, So. of
Baltimore st.
ECHBERGHER Wolfe, tanner, Old Town, North st.
ECKEL Philip, ---- , South side of Camdon st.
EDWARDS Jonathan & Co., dry good store, 31, Baltimore st.
EDWARDS ----, widow, Inn keeper, 81, South St. Bowley's wharf.
EDWARDS & CO. ---- , carpenters, 19, No. Gay St.
EDWARDS & ALLEN, printers of the Maryland Journal, 1, Light St.
EDWARDS Paul, painter, Old Town, Granby st.
EDWARDS William, sea captain, Carolina st. near Fell's Point.
EDWARDS & ARMSTRONG, dry good store, Old Town, 9, Bridge st.
EDWARDS James, dwelling, -- Old Town, -- 11, Bridge st.
EICHELBERGER Martin, weigh master, for the Port of Baltimore,
          dwelling, 40, South St.
EICHELBERGHER, junr. Jacob, saddler, 5, Cheapside
EICHELBERGHER George, dwelling, Triplets Alley.
EICHOFF Frederic, cordwainer, No. Charles St.
EICKLER Christian, carpenter, Eutau St.
EISLE John, drayman, Fell's Point, Pitt St.
EISELEN Conrad, merchant, dwelling, 25, Water St.
EISELEN & HORNE, merchants store & counting house, lower end of Mc'Clures
Wharf.
ELPHINSTON David, clerk, 59, No. Gay St.
ELVIN William, watchmaker, Fell's Point, 32, Thames St.
ELLICOT & Co. flour merchants, store and counting house, 41, Light St.
ELLICOT Benjamin, & James, flour merchants, store and counting house, 45,
Light St.
ELLICOT Elias, merchant, dwelling, 43, Pratt St.
ELLIOT Hardman, hack carriage keeper, 18, So. Howard St.
ELLIOT Benjamin, labourer, Old Town, North St.
ELLIOT Henry, carpenter, Carolina st. near Fell's Point.
ELLIS Thomas, inn keeper, Little York st. near the wind mill.
ELVVES(?) William, cabinet maker, 7, Nor. Liberty st.
EMICK Nicholas, carpenter, Nor. side of Camdon st.
EMI Philip, carman, Forrest st. Federal Hill.
ENDSOR John, Blacksmith, Fell's Point, Apple Alley.
ENGLES Silas, ship carpenter, Fell's Point, 31, Market st.
ENNALLS Andrew Skinner, merchant, store and counting house, 97, Sou. st.
Bowleys Wharf.

--- Do. --- dwelling 4, Sou. Gay st.
ENNISS, Joshua, house joiner, Fell's Point, 17, Market st.
ENNIS Philip, distiller, Old Town, Granby st.
ENNIS Stephen, taylor, Primrose Alley, between Light & Char. sts.
ENROSE James, cordwainer, Fell's Point, 4, Shakespears Alley.
ENSOR Martha, huckster, Fell's Point, 26, Queen st.
ENSOR William, clerk of lumber yard, Fell's Point, 26, Queen St.
ENSOR Abraham,   Old Town, Bridge St. beyond Winon St.
ERNEST Caleb, carpenter, 18, No. Frederic st.
ETCHBERGHER William, huckster, Fell's Point, 12, Thames st.
ETTING Shinah, widow, boarding house, 3, Baltimore st.
ETTING Solomon, merchant, 15, So. Calvert st.
ETTING Reuben, dwelling, East st. between Calvert and Gay sts.
ETTING & KENNEDY, milleners, 53, Baltimore st.
EVANS Thomas, boarding house, 135, Baltimore st.
EVANS William, Inn keeper, 187, Baltimore st.
EVANS George, dwelling,   240, Baltimore st.
EVANS John, baker, 64, South st.
EVANS & BAXLEY, grocery and flour store, 14, Cheapside.
EVANS Griffith, cooper, dwelling, 27, South Gay st.
EVANS John, pilot, Fell's Point, 6, Wilks st.
EVANS Mary, widow, seamstress, Old Town, Jones st.
EVANS Henry, bricklayer, Eden st. between Old Town and Fell's Point.
EVAHEART Jacob, carpenter, 54, Harrison St.
EVERHEART George, grave digger, Fish St.
EWALT John, drayman, Barre St. Federal Hill.
EXCHANGE & INSURANCE Office, 2, Commerce St.

FABRE Lewis Augustin, merchant, Fell's Point, 55, Market St.
FAGET John, boarding house, 12, Bank St.
FAIRFAX Stephen, labourer, Ruxton Lane, between Light and Charles St.
FALCONER and BLACKISTON, merchants store and counting house, 8, Bowleys Wharf.
FALCONER Abraham, merchant, dwelling 78, Hanover St.
FARIS William, looking glass factory, framer carver and gilder, 36, So.
Calvert St.
FARLAND Joseph, sea captain, Fell's Point, 24, Alisanna St.
FARNSWORTH James, cordwainer, Old Town, 35, Franch st.
FARRELL Timothy, drayman, passage between Waggon Alley and Fayette st.
FARRELL James, Inn keeper, Fell's Point, 1, Bond st.
FARRELL George, Inn keeper, Fell's Point, 14, Market st.
FAUBERT & FONBERTEAU, joiners, 45, No. Gay st.
FAUCHET Jean,   of St. Domingo, 51, North Howard st.
FAVERIE ---- , taylor, 22, Market place.
FEARSON Jesse, dry good store, Fell's Point, 3, Bond st.
FELLOW Henry, carman, Welcome Alley, Federal Hill.
FENBY Peter, huckster, Fell's Point, 45, Wilks st.
FENTON Thomas, house bell hanger, South side Second st.
FENNEL Chloe, washerwoman, Lombard st.
FERRALL James, wet good store, 62, South st.
FERGUSON William, merchant, 35, South st.
FEURIE Joseph, merchant, Old Town, Albermarle st.
FICKE Andrew, instrument maker, 79, No. Howard st.
FIELDS William, pilot, Fell's Point, 26, Alisanna st.
FIFE James,   Ruxton Lane, between Light & Charles st.
FIFER John, stage driver, 31, No. Gay st.
FIGUERE --- , of St. Domingo, Fell's Point, Strawbury Alley.

FIGUIERER Latapie & ROURNIER, boarding house, 6, Baltimore st.
FINLASS Sebastian, stay maker, 7, No. Frederic st.
FINLAY ----- , ware house, 14, Pratt st.
FINLAY Ebenezer, dwelling 20, No. Howard st.
FINLY John, mariner, Fell's Point, Lancaster Alley.
FINN William, carpenter & joiner, Old Town, Jones st.
FIRBY John, Inn keeper, Fell's Point, 18, Market st.
FISHBURN Philip, flour merchant, Fayette between Liberty and Howard st.
FISHER James, cordwainer, 8, Water st.
FISHER Robert, carpenter, 6, No. Calvert st.
FISHER John, currier, dwelling, No. 8, Calvert st.
FISHER Daniel, carpenter, 41, Pratt st.
FISHER Tobias, carpenter & joiner, East st. between Charles & Liberty sts.
FISHER Mary, widow, seamstress, Old Town, 32, So. High st.
FISHER John Denton, Old Town, 49, Wilks st.
FISHER Joseph, carpenter, Old Town, 9, French st.
FISHER John, carpenter, Montgomery st. Federal Hill.
FISHER George, Carpenter, Waggon Alley, between Howard & Liberty sts.
FISHWICK James, sail maker, Fell's Point, Ann st.
FITCH Henry, grocer, Old Town, 48, Bridge st.
FITZE John & William, coopers, shop, Fell's Point, 7, Philpot st.
--- Ditto   dwelling, Fell's Point, Wills st. between Philpot &
Queen sts.
FITZGERALD William, Inn keeper, Fell's Point, 10, Fells st.
FITZPATRICK Joseph Starch maker, No. Liberty st. West side.
FLAN Michael, sail maker, Fell's Point, 8, Queens st.
FLEMMING John, carpenter, Fell's Point, Queen st. So. side.
FLETCHER Philip, carpenter, Waggon Alley, between How'd and Eutau sts.
FLETCHER James, scowman, Old Town, Bridge str. beyond Winon str.
FLETZER Martin, carpenter, Lexington st. South side.
FLORENCE Joseph, wheelwright, Goodman st. Federal Hill.
FLOYD Charles, cordwainer, German st. between Howard and Eutau sts.
FLOYD Thomas & Caleb, potters, Fell's Point, 109, Bond st.
FLOYD Caleb, dwelling Old Town, 10, So. High st.
FOBLE Casper, Drayman, Eden st.
FOCKE Frederic & Co, merchants, 144, Baltimore st.
FONERDEN Adam, shoe warehouse, 54, Baltimore st.
FONERDEN Eliza, shoe store, 151, Baltimore st.
FORBES Elizabeth, widow, boarding house, Fell's Point, 17, Thames st.
FORD Edmund, Waggon Alley, between How'd & Eutau sts.
FORD Joseph,   , Fell's Point, Lancaster Alley,   East of Bond st.
FORD William, Inn keeper, upper Water st.
FORDNY William, cow-skin whip maker, Old Town, York st.
FOREMAN David, carpenter, South side Lexington st.
FOREMAN William, cordwainer, Old Town, 51, Bridge st.
FORNEY Peter, grocery & flour store, 235, Baltimore st.
FORSTER Nicholas, sea captain, Fell's Point, 96, Bond st.
FORSYTH Alexander, Inn keeper, 104, No. Howard st.
FORRESTER Stradford, drayman, Old Town, So. Green st.
FOSH John Michael, baker, Ruxton Lane, between Light and Charles sts.
FOSS George, stone quarrier, 78, No. Howard st.
FORTUNE James, ship baker, Fell's Point, 13, Philpot st.
FOWLER Margaret, widow, 58, No. Howard st.
FOWLER William, carman, Fell's Point, East side of Bond str. upper end.
FOWLER George, ship carpenter, Fell's Point, 37, Market st.
FOWLER Isaac, mariner, Fell's Point, Apple Alley.

FOWLER James, cordwainer, Fell's Point, Bond st.
FOWLER James, mariner, Carolina st. near Fell's Point.
FOXALL Thomas, grocer, North st. Log town.
--- Bitto   grocery store, 19, Second st.
FOY Eleanor, widow, seamstress, Fell's Point, 23, Bond st.
FRANCE Joseph, hack carriage keeper, German Lane, between Howard and Eutau sts.
FRAME Abraham, butcher, Old Town, Bridge str. beyond Winon sts.
FRAZIER James, sea captain, King George st.
FREDERICK Michael, labourer, Eutau st.
FREGNET Nicholas, of St. Domingo, 33, No. Gay st.
FRELET Claude Joseph, baker, Fell's Point, 5, Bond st.
FREIN James, labourer, Fell's Point, Alisanna st.
FRENCH Urah, widow, seamstress, South side Lexington st.
FRENCH Simon, pilot, Fell's Point, 10, Shakespears Alley.
FRENCH Dominic, butcher, Carolina st. near Fell's Point.
FREEBURGHER Henry, baker, 97, No. Howard st.
FREEMAN Samuel, schoolmaster, Waggon Alley, between How'd and Eutau sts.
FRICK Peter, china store, 9, So. Gay st.
--- Ditto   china store, 58, Baltimore st.
FRIDAY John, seine maker, South side Camdon st.
FROBES Christopher, joiner, Fayette, between Liberty and Howard sts.
FROGETT Richard, Barber, Primrose Alley, between Light and Charles sts.
FRY Andrew, cordwainer, German st. between Howard and Eutau sts.
FRY Samuel, carpenter, Sharp st.
FUGUERER   , of St. Domingo, Old Town, Jones st.
FULMER Elizabeth, seamstress, Fell's Point, 104, Bond st.
FULTZ William, cordwainer, No. side Camdon st.
FULLERTON Elizabeth, seamstress, Fell's Point, 24, Philpot st.
FULLWINER Magdalen, widow, West side of Nor. Liberty st.
FURLONG William, sea captain, Fell's Point, 5 Shakespears Alley.
FURNEY Joseph, tanner, Green st. No. of Baltimore st.
FURNEY John, rope maker, Barre st. Federal Hill.
FURNIVAL Alexander, post master, office and dwelling, 7, St. Pauls Lane.

GAINNIER Jean, cabinet maker, 17, Light st.
GALAND Jean Baptiste, taylor, 3, No. Gay st.
GALE Benjamin, carpenter, 83, Pratt st.
GALLAGHER Alexander, flour store, 254, Baltimore st.
GALLAWAY Thomas, carman, Fell's Point, Pitt st.
GALLAWAY William, grocer, Fell's Point, 48, Bond st.
GANTZ Adam, dry good store, 6, Pratt st.
GARDINER James, flour & grocery store, 31, No. Howard st.
GARDINER Julia, seamstress & washerwoman, German st. between Liberty and
Howard sts.
GARDINER John, schoolmaster, Fell's Point, Ann st.
GARDINER William, labourer, Fell's Point, Happy Alley.
GARDINER Timothy, sea captain, Fell's Point, 10, Queen st.
GARING Elizabeth, washerwoman, Barre st. Federal Hill.
GARLAND John, cordwainer, Fell's Point, Happy Alley.
GARMAN & HORN, grocers, 66, No. Howard st.
GARMAN John, stone cutter, 83, No. Howard st.
GARNEY John, bricklayer, Old Town, Albermarle st.
GARNIER Blaise, mason, Alley, between Light and Charles sts.
GARTS LE POLD & Co. sugar refiners, 9, Water st.
GARTS & Co.   distilling, So. side of Camdon st.
GARTS Peter, merchant, store & counting house, 79, South str. Bowleys Wharf

GARVAN Mathew, carpenter, 27, No. Gay st.
GATCHELL & TODD, merchants, Fell's Point, 5, Thames st.
GAUTIER ---- , of St. Domingo, Old Town, Low st.
GAUTIER --- , of   do.   Barre st. Federal Hill.
GEDDES David, revenue officer, Fell's Point, 8, Philpot st.
GERALD Samuel, hair dresser, Saratoga st.
GERISH Francis, carpenter, Old Town, 56, So. High st.
GERMAN James, labourer, South Frederic st.
GERMAN Peggy, widow, boarding house, 42, Pratt st.
GERNON Richard & John, merchant, dwelling 6, Commerce st.
--- Ditto ---   ware house, Commerce st. 28, McClures Wharf.
GHEQUIERE Charles, merchant, 157, Baltimore st.
--- Ditto ------   , wine store, 5, Charles st.
GETZ John, Physician, 15, So. Howard st.
GIBSON William, clerk of Baltimore County court, 20, South Gay st.
GIBSON James, carpenter, Old Town, Duke st.
GIBBERTHORN T. cordwainer, Fell's Point, 55, Bond st.
GIBBS John, waggoner, Fell's Point, Apple Alley.
GILBERT & BROWN, curriers, 2, Cheapside.
GILBERT Thomas P. do. dwelling, Old Town, 19, So. High st.
GILBERT Augustin, --- of St. Domingo, Old Town, South Green st.
GILES J. & William, merchants, 17, So. Calvert st.
GILMORE Robert & Co. merchants, dwelling, 35, Water st.
GILL Thomas, huckster, 63, No. Howard st.
GILL John, carpenter, Old Town, So. High st.
GILL Gabriel, bricklayer, Whisky Alley, between Howard and Eutau sts. So. of
Baltimore st.
GILLIARD Jacob, blacksmith, Old Town, Bridge st. beyond Winon st.
GILLISON John A. perfumer & hair dresser, 5, Nor. Liberty st.
GILLMEYER Francis, dry good & hardware store, 10. Nor. Howard st.
GIRAUD I. I. and Co. druggists & Chemists, 40, Baltimore st.
GIREAUD John James, surgeon and apothecary, Fell's Point, Bond st.
GISSE Peter, Inn keeper, Fell's Point, 14, Thames st.
GIST Cornelius Howard, deputy Clerk of Baltimore County Court, Boundary st.
GITTINGS & SMITH, merchants, 14, South Calvert st.
GITTINGS James, attorney at law, 51, Charles st.
GLACE Charles, 33, Harrison st.
GLEED James, mariner, Carolina st. near the Point.
GLEESON Morris, carrier of the Telegraphe, Nor. Charles st.
GOBERT Felix, hair dresser, 13, North gay st.
GOCHY Charles, mariner, Primrose Alley, between Light and Charles st.
GODWIN Lyde, Physician, 7, Nor. Gay st.
GODDARD Mary Catherine, book store, 80, Baltimore st.
GODDARD William, News Paper carrier, No. side of Lexing. st.
GODDARD ---, sea captain, King George st.
GOLD Peter, sea captain, 44, Charles st.
GOLDTHWAIT Samuel & Son, China & Liverpool ware store, 25, Sou. Calvert st.
--- Ditto ---   dry good store, 31, So. Calv. st.
GONNEL William, of St. Domingo, Saratoga st.
GOOD Eleanor, washerwoman, Eutau st.
GOODWIN William, dwelling East st. between Char. & Lib. st.
GOOLDEN John, ------ 28, Charles st.
GORDON John, saddle & harness maker, 79, Baltimore st.
   Ditto ------ dwelling, North st. Log Town.
GORDON John & William, merchants, store and counting house, 90, So. st. ---
Bowleys wharf

GORDON William, constable, East street between Calvert & Gay streets.
GORDON Michael, rigger, Fell's Point, Lancaster Alley.
GORDON John, mariner, Fell's Point, 4, Fleet st.
GORE Richard, dry good store, Fell's Point, 14, Thames st.
GORMLY Owens, --- , west side, North Liberty st.
GORSUCH Nicholas, --- , 31, No. Gay st.
GORSUCH Joshua, dry good store, Old Town, 60, Bridge st.
--- Ditto --- inn keeper, Old Town, 62, Bridge st.
GORSUCH --- , Sheriff's Office, 48, North Frederick st.
GOTTIER Edward, Cooper, Fell's Point, 18, Fells st.
GOUGH William, cordwainer, Nor. st. Log Town.
GOUGH Henry Dorsey, Old Town, Front st.
GOULD SMITH William, dry good store, 66, No. GRy st.
GOULDING John, sail maker, Fell's Point, 26, Market st.
GOY Mariette, of St. Domingo, Fell's Point, So. side Fleet st.
GRAFFLIN Jacob, sail maker, dwelling, 13, Pratt st.
GRAFFLIN Clopper and Hardeston, sail makers loft, end of M'Clures wharf.
GRAHAM John & Co. hardware store, 11, So. Calvert st.
GRALOT Catherine, Carolina st. near Fell's Point.
GRAMBERG John, carman, No. side, Camdon st.
GRANT Daniel, junr. & Hezekiah, merchts. store & count. house, 99, South st.
Bowleys wharf.
GRANT Daniel, --- 10, Light st.
GRANT Daniel, junr, dwelling, Old Town, Granby st.
GRANGER Joseph, Hostler, Alley, between Light and Charles sts.
GRANGER Daniel, mariner, Primrose Alley, between Light and Charles sts.
GRAPEVINE ·· , Grocery store, 76., No. Howard st.
GRAVE Frederic, labourer, Old Town, Franch st. Precinct.
GRAVES & ARNOLD, merchts. store and count. house, 78, South st. Bowleys wharf
GRAVES Ebenezer, grocery store, 8, So. Gay st.
GRAVES Nero, carman, Dutch Alley, between Howard and Liberty sts.
GRAY William, ship joiner, Fell's Point, So. side of Queen st.
GRAY Catherine, washerwoman, Fell's Point, East side of Bond st. upper end
GRAY Peter, taylor, Sharp st.
GRAY Ann, widow, millener, 50, Baltimore st.
GRAYBILL Philip, flour merchant, 177, Baltimore st.
GREANER Daniel, taylor, 52, Harrison st.
GREGORY David, carpenter, Old Town, 26, French st.
GREEB Conrad, cordwainer, 56, Harrison st.
GREEN Thomas, cordwainer, Bank st. near Fell's Point.
GREEN John, nail maker, Fell's Point, 26, Market st.
GREEN William, cordwainer, Fell's Point, 38, Fell's st.
GREEN Robert, sawyer, Fell's Point, Strawbury Alley.
GREEN --- , widow, 8, Hanover st.
GREENTREE Mathew, dry good store, 126, Baltimore st.
GRIEST Isaac, office, Fell's Point, 2, George st.
GRIFFIN Thomas, carpenter, 22, So. Howard st.
GRIFFIN Abraham, blacksmith, 40, Pratt st.
GRIFFITH Ely, carpenter, 13, So. Howard st.
GRIFFITH Nathan, Inn keeper, Old Town, 6, Bridge st.
GROCE Lewis, blacksmith, 46, Harrison st.
GROS Peggy, --- , widow, 36, Pratt st.
GROSE John, grocery store, 61, No. Gay st.
GROUT Paul & Co. grocery store, 108, Baltimore st.
GROOM William, mariner, Fell's Point, 91, Bond st.

GRUB Michael, cedar cooper, 230, Baltimore st.
GRUB Andrew, cedar cooper, 245, Baltimroe st.
--- Ditto ---   dwelling, Mc'Clemens Alley.
GRUBB Peter, carpenter, German street, between Liberty and Howard sts.
GRUNDY George, mercht. 136, Baltimore st.
GUFFEY Ann, widow, Old Town, Front st.
GUOERAN Isidore, slop(flop?) shop, 23, Light st.
GULLIDONS George, soap & tallow chandler, East st. between St. Pauls Lane and Charles st.
GUTTEROW Joseph, sea captain, 34, Charles st.
GUTTEROW John, wood corder, 38, Charles st.
GUTTRY Joshua, grocery store, 91, Hanover st.

HABLISTIN Barthelemy, hair dresser, and starch and hair powder maker, 49, South st.
HACKET --- , merchant, 10, No. Gay st.
HAGEN Mary, widow, Old Town, No. Winon st.
HAGEMEN Henry, carpenter, East str. between Charles and Liberty strs.
HAGERTY John, bookseller & stationer, 1, Water st.
HAGTHROP Edward, cordwainer, Fell's Point, 17, Fells st.
HAHN John Adam, store and Inn keeper, 58, Light st.
HAIFLIGH Frederic, house joiner, 24, So. Howard st.
HAINE John, oil miller, West side of So. Howard st.
HAINES Josiah, drayman, Dutch Alley, between Howard and Liberty strs.
HALES Robert, dry good store, Old Town, Bridge st. beyond Winon st.
HALEY Dennis, carpenter, Public Alley
HALFPENNY William, pilot, Fell's Point, Alisanna st.
HALMES John, Dutch fan maker, 42, Pratt st.
HALY Thomas, waterman, Fell's Point, 9, Alisanna st.
HALL William, glove and leather breeches maker, 194, Baltimore st.
HALL Philip, Inn keeper, 60, Light st.
HALL Caleb, dwelling, 79, Hanover st.
HALL Levi, grocery store, 5, County wharf.
HALL Edward, bellows maker, Waggon Alley, between Liberty and Howard sts.
HALL Benjamin, brick maker, Waggon Alley, between Howard and Liberty strs.
HALL Isaac & Leban, Fell's Point, Philpot str. Pattersons wharf.
HALL James, ship carpenter, Fell's Point, 43, Bond st.
HALL Isaac, ship carpenter, dwelling Fell's Point, 45, Bond st.
HALL George, house joiner, Fell's Point, 113, Bond st.
HALL Margaret, widow, seamstress, Fell's Point, 19, Market st.
HALL John, bricklayer, Fell's Point, 25, Alisanna st.
HALL Alexr. F. & Co. dry good store, Fell's Point, 8, Fells st.
HALL Jane, widow, Old Town, No. Green st.
HALL Edward, carman, Carolina st. near Fell's Point.
HALL Jonathan, sea captain, Fell's Point, 18, Bond st.
HALLICK Elizabeth, midwife, Old Town, Granby st.
HAMILTON John Agnew, paver, East st. between St. Pauls Lane, and Charles st.
HAMILTON John, revenue officer, Fell's Point, Wolf st.
HAMILTON William, pilot, Fell's Point, 30, Queen st.
HAMLYN John, at Mr. Coles, 4, South st.
HAMMER Frederic, dry good store, 39, So. Calvert st.
HAMMER Peter, taylor, Public Alley.
HAMMER Henry, upholsterer and paper hanger, Eutau St. No. of Baltimore St.
HAMMERSLY Thomas, copper smith and tinman, 236, Baltimore st.
    Ditto,   dwelling, 14, No. Liberty st.
HAMMERSLY sen. Thomas, copper smith and tinman, Dutch Alley between Howard and Eutau sts.

HAMMOND John, merchant, 8, Hanover st.
HAMMOND Thomas, taylor, 9, Market Place st.
HAMMOND Harriet, 59, Pratt st.
HAMMOND Isaac, overseer of wheelbarrow men, No. side of Lexington st.
HAND Henry, drayman, Forrest st. Federal Hill.
HAND and BARBER, portrait painters, gilders and glaziers, upper end of Balt-
imore st. between Eutau and Green sts.
HANENGER Catharine, widow, 58,No. Howard st.
Hansman Samuel, butcher, Carolina st. near Fell's Point.
HANNAH Caleb, windsor chair maker, 7 Cheapside.
    Ditto,   ditto, Fell's Point, 32, Wilks st.
HANNAH William, dwelling, 93, Pratt st.
HANNER Grizelda,   Forrest Lane.
HANNICKER Jacob, cordwainer, Sharp st.
HAPFIELD Henry, painter, Fell's point, 21, Fells st.
HARDING Christopher, carpenter, So. side Lexington st.
HARDISTER Benjamin, sail maker, Fell's Point, Pettycoat Lane.
HARDIVILLIER ---, merchant of St. Domingo, Gough st. near Fell's Point.
HARDY James, rigger, Fell's Point, 44, Alisanna st.
HARGOOD Henry, brickmaker, Fell's Point, West side of Bond str. upper end.
HARKER John, Baker, Old Town, Bridge st. beyond Winon str.
HARMAN Daniel, carpenter, 83, Pratt st.
HARMAN Philip, carpenter, Waggon Alley, West of How'd st.
HARPER Samuel, leather breeches maker, Old Town, 13, South High st.
HARRIS William, cabinet maker, 8, No. Frederic st.
HARRIS Moses, labourer, Old Town, North st.
HARRIS Prince, labourer, Waggon Alley, West of Howard st.
HARRIS David, cashier of the Branch Bank of the United States, 1, No. Gay st.
HARRISON William, merchant, 84, Baltimore st.
HARRISON Jonathan, house joiner, Fell's Point, 119, Bond st.
----Ditto ---, grocery store, Fell's Point, 42, Fells st.
HARRISON Thomas, carpenter, Fell's Point, Lancaster Alley, West of Bond st.
HARRISON Phebe, washerwoman, Fell's Point, Lancaster Alley, East of Bond st.
HARRISON Edward, carpenter, Fell's Point, Stawberry Alley.
HARSHMAN Sarah, widow, seamstress, Old Town, No. Winon st.
HART John,   15, No. Gay st.
HART Lewis, dry good and grocery store, 25, No. Howard st.
HARTMAN Paul, dry good store, 79, Baltimore st.
HARTMAN Jacob, shoe last maker, Old Town, Duke st.
HARTNETT James, taylor, 79, Water st.
HARWOOD I.   Fell's Point, 15, Fell's st.
HARWOOD Rachel, millener, 16, Charles st.
HASLET Moses, physician, 56, No. Gay st.
HASTINGS Mary, widow, boarding house, Eden st. near Jones' Falls.
HASSAFRAS George, carpenter, 42, No. Frederic st.
HASSAM Josiah, painter, Fell's Point, Strawberry Alley.
HASSARD William, grocery store, 67, No. Howard st.
HASSARD Bridget, widow, Goodman st. Federal Hill.
HASSARD William, taylor, Goodman st. Federal Hill.
HASSET William, taylor, Honey Alley, Federal Hill.
HATHAWAY Jethro, mariner, Fell's Point, 4, Shakespears Alley.
HATTON John, shop keeper, boarding house, Eden st. near Jones's Falls
HAWKINS John, taylor, Fell's Point, 6, Fells st.
--- Ditto --- Fell's Point, 15, Fleet st.
HAWKINS William, taylor, 7, South st.

HAY John,   Fell's Point, 37, George st.
HAY John, carpenter, Whiskey Alley, between Howard and Eutau strs. So. of
Baltimore st.
HAY Jacob, carpenter, Whiskey Alley, between Howard and Eutau strs. So. of
Baltimore st.
HAY George, harness maker and trimmer, Bottle Alley, between Howard and
Eutau strs. So. of Baltimore st.
--- Ditto ---, shop, Second st. between Gay st. and the Falls.
HAYES junr. William, Physician, Fell's Point, 40, Philpot st.
HAYES John, painter, Old Town, 37, Front st.
HAYWARD Roche and Co. grocery store, 45, So. Calvert st.
HAYWARD Benjamin, joiner, So. side of Cambdon st.
HEALY Peter, Inn keeper, Fell's Point, 7, Bond st.
HEALY John, silk dyer, 40, No. Frederic st.
HEART Sarah, washerwoman, 77, Harrison st.
HEATH James, taylor, Fell's Point, 27, Fells st.
HEATHCOTE and DALL, merchants. 74, Baltimore st.
HEFFER Peter, Inn keeper, 64, No. Howard st.
HEIDE George, grocery store, 163, Baltimore st.
--- Ditto   oil and colour store, 23, Sou. Calvert st.
HEIDE and KIPP, oil and colour store, 16, Cheapside.
HEIDE Philip,   Lombard st.
HEIMS Solomon, inn keeper, Montgomery st. Federal Hill.
HEINECKE   physician, 75, Pratt st.
HEINER Esther, widow,   Sharp st.
HEINZMAN Samuel, butcher, Carolina st. near Fell's Point.
HEITMAN John, taylor, Saratoga st.
HOLLEN John, labourer, Eden st. near Jones's Falls.
HENDERSON William, plaisterer, Saratoga st.
HENDRICKSON Joseph, taylor, 24, Charles st.
HENNAMAN John, coachmaker, 17, So. Howard st.
HENNINGER George, hog butcher, 46, No. Gay st.
HENRY Rosanna, widow, So. Liberty st.
HENRY Daniel, merchant, Forrest Lane.
HENRY Christian, widow, Carolina St. near Fell's Point.
HEPWELL Humphrey, taylor, Alley between St. Pauls Lane and No. Calvert St.
HERAUD Louis, of St. Domingo, Old Town, So. High St.
HERNER John, bricklayer, Forrest Lane.
HEROD Henry, rigger, Fell's Point, Apple Alley, between Alisanna and Fleet st.
HEROD Margaret, widow, schoolmistress, Triplets Alley.
HEROL Robert, carpenter, 29, No. Gay st.
HERR Peter, baker, 181, Baltimore st.
HERRING Langford, gorcery store, 209, Baltimore st.
HERRING Ludwic, carpenter, Old Town, Albermarle st.
HERSHBERGER Adam, rope maker, 32, So. Howard st.
HESLIP John, cordwainer, Conowago st.
HESSINGTON William, stone cutter, Welcome Alley, Federal Hill.
HETHERINGTON Thomas, drayman, Waggon Alley, West of Howard st.
HETTINGER Michael, labourer, Old Town, Stigers Lane.
HEWITT Caleb, tobacconist, 226, Baltimore st.
HICKS James, boarding house, Old Town, 5, So. High st.
HICKS & LAW, cabinet makers, Old Town, 7, So. High st.
HICKS Tamor, eating house, Front st. West of Calvert st.
HICKLEY Samuel, burr mill stone maker, Cow-pen Lane.
HICKSON Thomas, dry good store, 111, Baltimore st.

HIGGINS Eleanor, spinstress, No. Liberty st.
HIGGINS John, mariner, Fell's Point, 123, Bond st.
HIGGINS Patrick, pedlar, Old Town, No. Green st.
HIGHJOE Elizabeth, widow, 101, Nor. Howard st.
HILDEBRAND Jacob,   South Frederic st.
HILL Anthony, cordwainer, Upper Water st.
HILL John Button(?), carpenter, New Church st.

HILL William, mariner, Fell's Point, Apple Alley, between Alisanna and Fleet
sts.
HILL Thomas, plaisterer, passage back of St. Pauls Lane
HILL James   do.   do.   do.
HILLBUT John, butcher, East st. between Charles and Liberty st.
HILLEN John, leather and grocery store, 23, Water st.
HINKS Mary, retail shop, 93, Nor. Howard st.
HINTON Nebo, ship carpenter, Fell's Point, Alisanna st.
HINTZE Charles, physician, 17, Second st.
HIREY John, butcher, Waggon Alley, west of Howard st.
HYNER Joseph, carman, Old Town, Stigers Lane.
HOBART Frederic, carpenter, 98, Pratt st.
HOBBS James, mathematical instrument maker, Old Town, So. Green st.
HOBURG Conrad, cordial distiller, Old Town, Stigers Lane.
HODGSON Nicholson & Co. merchant, 152, Baltimore st.
HODGSON Robert, dwelling 70, Hanover st.
HOFFMAN Peter and Co. dry good store, 53, Baltimore st.
HOFFMAN George, merchant, 4, So. Calvert st.
HOFFMAN Peter and Son, merchants, 18, So. Calvert st.
HOFFMAN and SCHRYER, curriers, 9, Cheap side.
HOFFMAN Jacob, dwelling, 46, Hanover st.
    Ditto,   grocery store, 51,   do.
HOFFMAN Henry, taylor, Fayette between Howard and Eutau sts.
HOFFMAN Andrew, shingle dresser, Old Town, French st. Precinct.
HOFFMAN Daniel, butcher, Cyder Alley So. of Baltimore st.
HOFFMAN Henry, carpenter, Paca st.
HOGANS Richard, Lee st. Federal Hill.
HOGAN Patrick, grocer, Fell's Point. 47, Bond st.
HOGMAN John, Tinman, Waggon Alley, between Howard and Liberty sts.
HOLLAND Silvester, labourer, No. Liberty st.
HOLLAND John, mariner, Fell's Point, Argyle Alley.
HOLLIN John, carman, Old Town, 57, Bridge st.
HOLLINS John, merchant, dwelling and counting house, 39, So. Gay st.
HOLLINGSWORTH Thomas and Samuel, merchants, counting house and flour store,
41, So. Calvert st.
HOLLINGSWORTH Thomas, dwelling, 15, South st.
HOLLINGSWORTH Samuel, dwelling, 8, South st.
HOLLINGSWORTH Jesse, merchant, store and counting house, 8, County Wharf.
    Ditto,   dwelling, 14, Bank st.
HOLLINGSWORTH Zebulon, attorney at law, 5, Nor. Calvert st.
HOLLINGSWORTH Henry, Revenue Officer, Fell's Point, Strawberry Alley.
HOLLOWAY Henry, blue dyer, Sharp st.
HOLMES James, waterman, Carolina st. near Fell's Point.
HOLMES John, merchant, store and counting house, 169, Bal. st.
    Ditto   dwelling, 13, Charles st.
HOLMES James, dutch fan maker, Ruxton Lane, between Light and Charles st.
HONICOMBE John, baker, Old Town, 27, Bridge st.
HOLTON William, plaisterer, Fell's Point, Strawberry Alley.
HOLTON John, plaisterer,   do.   do.

HOOBER George, painter and glazier, Fayette st. between Howard and Eutau st.
HOOK Michael, coach maker, 57, Charles st.
HOOK Ferdinand, wheelwright, 90, Charles st.
HOOK Joseph, saddler and harness maker, Eutau st.
HOOPER William, --- , Old Town, Bridge st. beyond Winon street.
HOPE James, dwelling, North side Camdon st.
HOPKINS Gerrard, cabinet maker, 39, Nor. Gay st.
    Ditto ---, grocery store, 43, South Calvert st.
HOPKINS Nicholas, sea captain, Fell's Point, Ann st. between Pitt and
Alisanna streets.
HOPKINS James, grocer, Baltimore st. between Eut. and Green.
HORMAN John, wheelwright, Boundary st.
HORN Philip, butcher and sausage maker, 35, Nor. Howard st.
HORN John, wheelwright, Old Town, 74, South High st.
HORNBY William, cabinet maker, Old Town, Nor. Green st.
HORNBY Gualter, cabinet maker, 6, Light st.
HORNER Nathan, carpenter, Old Town, 18, South High st.
HOSS Frederic, inn Keeper, Lombard street.
HOSS John, retail shop, 11, South Howard street.
HOSSMAN John, taylor, Fell's Point, 16, Queen st.
HOUSE John, cedar cooper, Fell's Point, 7, Alisanna st.
HOUSER George, inn keeper, Old Town, 50, Bridge st.
HOWARD George, carpenter, Old Town, Duke st.
HOWARD Joshua, cordwainer, Old Town, South Green st.
HOWARD Richard, tavern and boarding house, Fell's Point, 25 Bond street.
HOWARD John, bricklayer, Nor. side of Camdon st.
HOW Catherine, widow, seamstress, German st. between Howard and Eutau sts.
HOWELL James, ship carpenter, Fell's Point, Ann st. between Pitt and Alisanna
streets.
HOWELL John, store, 107 Hanover street.
HOWLAND Daniel, sea captain, South Frederic Street.
HOY Samuel, blockmaker, Fell's Point, Argyle Alley.
HOY John, shipcarpenter, Fell's Point, Alisanna st.
HUBON Senr. ----, South Howard st.
HUBON Stephen grocery and flour store, 75, Nor. Howard st.
HUDSON Margaret, widow, 171, Baltimore st.
HUDSON Robert, carpenter, 29, South Howard st.
HUDSON William Stevedore, Carolina st. near Fell's Point.
HUGHES Christopher,   Forrest st. Federal Hill.
HUGHES Mary, widow, Bank st. near Fell's Point
HUGHES Hannah, bonnet maker, 137, Baltimore st.
HUGHES William, sea captain, So. Pratt st.
HUGG Jacob, tanner, No. side Camdon st.
HUGO Thomas, revenue officer, Fell's Point, 3, George st.
HULSE Matthew, blacksmith, Fell's Point, 9, Alisanna st.
HULL John, butcher, 25, Harrison st.
HULL Fortune, ship carpenter, Fell's Point, Alisanna st.
HUMPHRY David, --- , Fell's Point, Alisanna st.
HUMPHRYS James, carman, Fell's Point, Alisanna st.
HUNT James, grocery store, Fell's Point, 10, Thames st.
HUNT Elizabeth, seamstress, Fell's Point, West side of Bond st. upper end.
HUNTER and LONG, grocery store, 43, Baltimore st.
HUSH Conrad, blacksmith, German st. between Liberty and Howard sts.
HUSKEY John, rigger, Fell's Point, Argyle Alley.
HUST John, labourer, Fell's Point, Lancaster Alley, East of Bond st.
HUSLEY George, tanner, Exeter st. near Old Town.

HUSSEY Nathaniel, inn keeper, 7, No. Howard st.
HUSSEY and Fisher, curriers, 3, Cheap side.
HUTCHINS Catherine, widow, inn keeper, 2, Bank st.
HUTCHINSON Thomas, labourer, Alley, between Light and Charles sts.
HUTTON James, grocery store, 22, Baltimore st.
HUTTON William   101, No. Howard st.
HUTTON and COLSTON, bakers, 10, Market Place st.
HUTTON Rebecca, washerwoman, Old Town, Stigers Lane.

JACKSON George, butcher, Old Town, French st. Precinct.
JACKSON Isaiah, carpenter, Old Town, 37, South High st.
JACKSON John, mariner, Fell's Point, Apple Alley.
JACKSON William, block and pump maker, Fell's Point, 11, Philpot st.
JACOBS Moses, dry good store, 83, Baltimore st.
JACOBS Samuel, taylor, 34, So. Calvert st.
JACOBS Joseph, hack carriage keeper, 10, So. Gay st.
JACOBS Bartholomey, carman, So. side Camdon st.
JACOB Simon, labourer, So. Howard st.
JACOB Patty, washerwoman, Eutau st.
JACOB William, sail maker, Fell's Point, 11, Market st.
JAFFRAY James, merchant, dwelling 92, Hanover st.
JALLAND John, inn keeper, Fell's Point, 54, Wilks st.
JAMES Tudor, dry good store, 232, Baltimore st.
JAMES and AMOS, flour store, 22, Cheap Side.
--- Ditto   warehouse 48, Light st.
JAMES George, labourer, Waggon Alley, between Howard and Liberty sts.
JAMES Henriette, widow, 5, No. Liberty st.
JAMES John, cooper, Forrest Lane.
JAMES John, mariner, Fell's Point, 11, George st.
JAMES William, inn keeper, Fell's Point, 30, Bond st.
JAMES John, cabinet maker, Old Town, Albermarle st.
JAMES Samuel,   Old Town,   do.
JAMES Jean Baptiste, jeweller, lapidary and engraver of Paris, 15, No. Gay st.
JAMISON Mary, widow, dwelling, So. Liberty st.
JANDIN Rosydine, widow, 23, Charles st.
JANIN   of St. Domingo, 70, Charles st.
JARRET Jean Joseph, cordwainer, 52, No. Gay st.
JARREL Moses, labourer, Eutau st.
JEFFERSON William, mariner, Dutch Alley, between Howard and Eutau sts.
JEFFRAYS James, mariner, Waggon Alley, between Howard and Eutau sts.
JEFFRIES John, drayman, Saratoga st.
JEFFRY Benjamin, drayman, Old Town, Bridge st. beyond Winon st.
JEMMISEN Joseph, carpenter, 42, No. Frederic st.
JENKINS Edward, saddler and Harness maker, 37, So. Calvert st.
JENKINS Thomas C. dry good store, 12, So. Calvert st.
JENKINS Philip, mariner, Fell's Point, Strawberry Alley.
JENKINS Thomas, dry good store, Fell's Point, 30, FNll's st.
JENNINGS Peter, mariner, Fell's Point, Apple Alley.
JENNINGS John, clerk,   So. Liberty st.
JENNY Nathaniel, sea captain, Fell's Point, 12, Queen st.
JESSOP Abraham, grocery store, 9, No. Howard st.
JEFFRO John, grocer, Fell's Point, 25, Wilks;
JENVEUVE   Carolina st. near Fell's Point.
ILGERE Mary, widow, seamstress, 74, Charles st.
INLO Joshua, carpenter, Fell's Point, 77, Bond st.
INLO Elizabeth, widow, Fell's point, 81, Bond st.
JOHN Hill, labourer, Fell's Point, Strawberry Alley.

JOHNS Richard, sea captain, Fell's Point, 28, Bond st.
JOHNS John, stage driver, Carolina st. near Fell's Point.
JOHNS Hosier, clerk, at Mrs. Slade's, M'Clelens Alley
JOHNS William, pilot, Fell's Point, Ann st.
JOHNS Isaac, cabinet maker, 25, No. Gay st.
JOHNSTON Christopher, merchant, 199, Baltimore st.
JOHNSTON Samuel, attorney at law, 33, Hanover st.
JOHNSTON Edward, physician and accoucheur, 93, Hanover st.
JOHNSTON Nicholas, labourer, Saratoga st.
JOHNSTON John, retail shop, North st. Log Town
JOHNSTON Joshua, portrait painter, German st. between Hanover and Howard sts.
JOHNSTON Sarah widow, Fell's Point, 17, Fleet st.
JOHNSTON William, sail maker, Fell's Point, 26, Thames st.
JOHNSTON James, taylor, Fell's Point, 34, Thames st.
JOHNSTON Joseph, bricklayer, Old Town, Bridge st. beyond winon street.
JOHNSTON Mathew, bricklayer, Old Town, Front st.
JOHNSTON Edward, dwelling, King George street.
JOHNSTON Thomas, physician, Bank street, between Light and Charles streets.
JOHNSTON Peter, mariner, Eutau street.
JOHONNOT George, merchant, store and counting house, 6, Bowleys Wharf.
JOHONNOT Francis, distiller, Old Town, Albermarle street.
JOLLY and VAN-BIBBER, gry good store, 28, So. Calvert Street
JOLLY and COS, grocery store, 50, Light street.
JONES Richard, painter and glazier, 32, So. Calvert street.
      Ditto oil and colour store, Fell's Point, 18, Philpot street.
JONES and JENKINS, tanners and curriers, 4, Water street.
JONES Aubrey, cordwainer, 32, No. Gay street.
JONES William, mason and bricklayer, 4, North Liberty street.
JONES William, bricklayer, Eutau street.
JONES Michael, plaisterer, Old Town, Bridge st. beyond Winon st.
JONES Benjamin, bricklayer, Old Town, Duke st.
JONES William, cordwainer, 77, Harrison st.
JOUBERT Peter, of St. Domingo, Barre st. Federal Hill.
JOYCE Peirce, carpenter, 27, No. Gay st.
JOYCE Ann, widow, Fell's Point, Argyle Alley.
JOYCE Joseph, carpenter, Old Town, Pitt st.
IRELAND Edward, dwelling, 38, South st.
--- Ditto   warehouse, Mc'Clures Wharf.
IRVIN Mark Henry, revenue officer, Fell's Point, So. side Fleet st.
IRVIN Rebecca, widow, seamstress, Old Town, Bridge st.
ITZCHKIN Philip, hack carriage driver, 203, Baltimore st.
JULIAN Joseph,   Fell's Point, 54, Wilks st.
JULIEN Marie Louisse, widow, of St. Domingo, King George st.
JUNEA Bernard, retail shop, 69, No. Howard st.
JUSTICE Joseph, taylor, dwelling, Old Town, 39, Bridge st.
--- Ditto   taylors shop, 80, Baltimore st.
IVARY Mathias, baker, Fell's Point, 17, Pitt st.

KAKN   , 56, No. Howard st.
KARG Catherine, seamstress, 43, No. Gay st.
KAUFFMAN   , joiner, So. side of Camdon st.
KAUN Alexander, rigger, Fell's Point, 6, Fleet st.
KEATINGE George, bookseller, 149, Baltimore st.
KEATINGE Henry, bookseller, book binder & circulation Library, 223, Baltimore
st.
KENTON William, sail maker, Fell's Point, 11, Pitt st.

KEATON Thomas, cordwainer, Fell's Point, 38, Bond st.
KEAN Edmund, cordwainer, 4, Cheapside.
KEAN Michael,   , Fell's Point, 16, Bond st.
KEARY James, merchant, Sharp st.
KEEBLE Humphery, pilot, Fell's Point, Wolf st.
KEENER Melchior, merchant, 208, Baltimore st.
KEENER Christian, merchant, 210, Baltimore st.
KEENER Michael, carpenter, So. Frederic st.
KEENER Peter & John, gun smiths, Old Town, No. Green st.
KEEN William, carpenter, 116, No. Howard st.
KEEPORT George P. notary public, 15, So. Gay st
KEERL Henry, physician, 231, Baltimore st.
KEILHOTS John, baker, 14, No. Howard st.
KELLENBERGER George, dry good store, 238, Baltimore st.
KELL Isaac, dry good store, 52, Baltimore st.
KELLER John, plane maker, Old Town, Stigers Lane.
KELLY Robert, shoe store, 68, Baltimore st.
KELLY Patrick, carpenter, 27, No. Gay st.
KELLY Patrick, carpenter, Fell's Point, 37, Wilks st.
KELLY Andrew, huckster, Fell's Point, 43, Wilks st.
KELLY Sarah, seamstress, Fell's Point, 28, Wilks st.
KELLY John, potter, Old Town, No. Winon st.
KELP John, labourer, Old Town, So. High st.
KELTHIMER Francis, carman, Saratoga st.
KELSO Thomas, merchant, 11, County Wharf.
KELSO John & George,   , Old Town, 43, So. High st.
KELSO Mary, widow, King George st. near Old Town.
KELTZER George, cordwainer, Old Town, No. Green st.
KEMELMEYER Frederic, Limner, 60, No. Gay st.
KEMPS Adam, carpenter, North st. Log Town.
KENDAL & KERR, brewery, Hanover st.
KENNEDY Anthony, John & Co. merchants, 172, Baltimore st.
KENNEDY Arthur, Irish linnen warehouse, 2, No. Gay st.
KENNEDY Robert, carpenter, Fell's Point, Strawberry Alley
KENNEDY Araienah(?),   Old Town, 36, French st.
KENT & MIDDLETON, tea warehouse, 127, Baltimore st.
KENT Emanuel, dwelling, 32, Hanover st.
KENT Robert, dry good store, 37, Baltimore st.
KENSEL Frederic, hair dresser & perfumer, 147, Baltimore st.
KEPLER John, grocer, Second st. between Gay st. and the Falls.
KER John, carpenter, Old Town, Albermarle st.
KERR John, schoolmaster, So. Liberty st.
KEY James, clark, Triplets Alley.
KEYSER Derrick, dwelling, 103, No. Howard st.
--- Ditto   grocery store, 17, Cheapside.
KEYSLER Catherine, widow, Old Town, 92, So. High st.
KHUNTZ Jacob cordwainer, Forrest Lane.
KHYME Frederic, butcher, Montgomery st. Federal Hill.
KISLE Nicholas, carpenter, German st. between Howard and Eutau sts.
KILLBREATH Thomas, drayman, So. Liberty st.
KILLEN John, dry good store, 75, Baltimore st.
KILTY John, supervisor for Maryland, office and Dwelling, 7, So. Howard st.
KIMBLE Henry, drayman, Paca st.
KIMERLY Jacob, labourer, Fell's Point, Happy Alley
KIMMEL & DECKER, flour and grocery store, 24, No. Howard st.

KIMPFF Jacob, retail shop, 28, No. Liberty st.
KING Jacob, combmaker, Conowago st.
KING Margaret, widow, No. side of Lexington st.
KING George, butcher, Dutch Alley, between Howard and Liberty st.
KING Elias, carpenter, German st. between Liberty and Howard sts.
KING Thomas, carpenter, Lombard st.
KING Mary, widow, Fell's Point, Strawberry Alley.
KING John, carpenter, Fell's Point, Strawberry Alley.
KING Benjamin, plumber, Fell's Point, 40, Fell's st.
KING Richard, whip sawyer, Brioy Alley, Federal Hill
KINSEL Jacob, bricklayer, Old Town, North st.
KIPP John, carman, 44, Pratt st.
KIPPS Nicholas, bricklayer, Eutau st. So. of Baltimore st.
KIRBY William, hard ware store, 30, Calvert st.
KIRBY William, grocery store, Fell's Point, 4, George st.
KISLER George, carpenter, Saratoga st.
KITZER Casper, hair dresser, Old Town, French st. pricincts.
KNAB & KRAWS, taylors, 46, South st.
KNAP Samuel, sea captain, Fell's Point, 34, Bond st.
KNICHT John, Godfried, gun & lock smith, So. side Lexington st.
KNIGHT Joshua, carpenter, 16, So. Howard st.
KNOX George, porter bottler, Fell's Point, 14, Philpot st.
KIFFMAN Abraham, inn keeper, 4, No. Gay st.
KONIG LIGETTE & Co. merchants, 212, Baltimore st.
KONIG August, merchant, 12, No. Howard st.
KRAWS George, baker, upper Water st.
KREAUSE John, cordwainer, 10, So. Howard st.
KREMS Joseph, taylor, 91, Baltimore street.
KREPS Michael, brickmaker, Fell's Point, Ann Street
KREUSE Christopher, overseer of the harbour machine, 101, Pratt street.
KURTZ Michael, baker, Fayette street, between Liberty and Howard streets.
KURTZ Daniel, clergyman, Lemmons Alley.
KUSACK Roger, mariner, Fell's Point, West side of Bond street, upper end.
KYRMS Charles, mariner, Fell's Point, 15, Shakespears Alley.

LABAT John, joiner, Fell's Point, 37, Bond street.
LA BORD Bernard, sea captain, 49, Charles street.
LA BORDE Joseph, painter & glazier, Fell's Point, 27, Wilks st.
LACASSAGNE   , Fell's Point, 12, Fleet street.
LACAZE   , physician, 20, Charles street.
LACOMBE   , young ladie's boarding school, 36, South street.
LACROIX Raymond, cordwainer, 52, No. Gay street.
LAFIT   , Old Town, 83, So. High street.
LAFRUIT Magdalen, widow, 32, Charles street.
LAHE   , dry good store, Primrose Alley, between Light and Charles
streets.
LAHMANN Martha, widow, 110, Hanover street.
LALLIER Jeanne, widow, of St. Comingo, Conway street, Federal Hill.
LAMBERT Victoire, Old Town, So. High street.
LAMDIN Thomas, ship carpenter, Fell's Point, Apple Alley.
LAMOTTE Daniel, tanner, Green street, No. Baltimore street.
LADRIEVE Anthony Gilis, Old Town, So. Green street.
LANGWORTHY Edward, clerk of the custom house, Fell's Point, West side of Bond
street, upper end.
LANNAY Louis, starch maker, Fell's Point, 67, Bond street.
LA PERIERE   , of St. Domingo, Physician, 51, No. Howard street.

LA PLAINE Jean Jacques, baker, So. side, Camdon street.
LA PLAS Joseph, stucco plaisterer, So. Howard street.
LAPPIN Biddy, widow, huckster, 20, So. Howard street.
LARNAR John, Carpenter, at Nathan Gavins, Second street, between Gay street,
and the Falls.
LASSINGUE peter, of St. Domingo, Lee stree, Federal Hill.
LATIL Joseph, dwelling 25, Charles street.
LATIL & TUREAUD, merchants, store and counting house, 67, South street, Bow-
leys Wharf.
LATOUCHE James William, sea captain, 35, Charles street.
LAUDERMAN Frederic, tobacconist, Fell's Point, 19, Bond street.
LAUTAUR Samuel, blacksmith, Old Town, Duke street.
LAW James & Co. merchants, 108, Baltimore street.
LAWRENCE Jacob, nailor, Old Town, Duke street.
LAWRENCE Richard, blacksmith, Fell's Point, 22, Fells street.
LAWRENCE Peter, mariner, Alley between Light and Charles st.
LAWRENCE John, tallow chandler & inn keeper, Fell's Point, 13, Fells street.
LAWRENCE Richard, anchor smith, Fell's Point, 7, Thames st.
LAWSON Richard, merchant and distiller, Old Town, Albemarle street
LAWSON Alexander, East street, between Calvert and Gay street.
LAY POLD John, dwelling, 103, Hanover street.
LAZARE Lawrent, waterman, 53, Charles street.
LEAGUE John, inn keeper, Fell's Point, 42, Bond street.
LEAGUE Thomas, constable, Old Town, No. Winon street.
LEAGUE Reuben, windsor chair maker, Bank street, between Light and Charles
street.
LEACHEY John, cooper, Triplets Alley.
LEAKIN Elizabeth, widow, Old Town, 55, Bridge street.
LEAKIN James, taylor, Old Town, 55, Bridge street.
LEARY Andrew, black and white smith, Hanover st.
LEAVLY Catherine, widow, boarding house, 29, No. Gay st.
LE BATARD Jean Louis, joiner, 13, Light st.
LEBEROU Anthony, hair dresser, Upper Water st.
LE BON Anniesse, of St. Domingo, 30, Charles st.
LE CAUS ----- carpenter, Fell's Point, 38, Bond st.
LE CLERE Francois, of St. Domingo, Waggon Alley, between Eutau and Howard sts.
LE COQ Jean, cooper, 15, Light st.
LE DUC Lawrence, grocer, Fell's Point, 34, Fell's st.
LE DOULX --- , confectioner, 24, Harrison st.
LEE Michael, waggoner, Public Alley.
LEE John, ship carpenter, Fell's Point, 40, Bond st.
LEE Joh, cooper, 48, Pratt st.
LEE Samuel, cabinet maker, 37, No. Gay st.
LEEKE Nicholas, schoolmaster, Fell's Point, 22, Alisanna st.
LEESON Francis, nailor, Fell's Point, Argyle Alley.
LEFEVRE Philip, cordwainer, 56, Harrison st.
LESTON William, carpenter, Fell's Point, Ann st.
LE GARDE Joseph, Old Town, 45, So. High st.
LEGER Gill Pascal, of St. Domingo, Old Town, 33, French st.
LE GRAS John Francis, dwelling, 1, St. Pauls Lane.
LEHAULT Joseph, cooper, Triplets Alley.
LEIGFRED Kathroul, widow, huckster, So. side of Lexington st.
LEMANE Joseph, cowdwainer, Public Alley.
LEMMON Joshua, dwelling, 29, So. Calvert st.
LEMMON and LEVERING, merchants, store and counting house, 28, Cheapside.

L'ENGLE John and Co. grocers, Old Town, 1, Bridge, st.
LENHARD Frederic, retail shop, 65, No. Howard st.
LENHART Henry, blacksmith, German st. between Howard and Eutau sts.
LENHART Jacob, blacksmith, do.   do.
LA PAGE Vigie, grocery store, 42, Baltimore st.
LA POLD Ludwic, King George st. near Old Town.
LE RET Peter, jeweller, New Church st.
    Ditto,   gold and silversmiths shop, 114, Baltimore st.
LEREW Abraham and George, carpenters, 113, No. Howard st.
LEREW James, taylor, 113, No. Howard st.
LE ROY ---, widow, Fell's Point, 110, Bond st.
LESEA ---, 2 No. Frederic st.
LESLIE Robert and Co. clock and watchmakers, 119, Baltimore st.
LESTER William, cordwainer, Old Town, Low st.
LEUDER Francoisse, widow, shop keeper, 68, Charles st.
LEVELY George, watch and clock maker, 140 Baltimore street.
LEVERING Enoch, grocery store, 32, Cheapside.
LEVERING Jesse, dwelling, 60, Hanover street.
LEVERING Nathan, flour and grocery store, 13, County Wharf.
LEVINGSTON ---, dry good store, Fell's Point, 46, Fell's street.
LEVINGSTON Paul,   Public Alley.
LEVY Jacob, broker, store and dwelling, 242, Baltimore street.
LEWIS Richard, dry good store, 33, Baltimore street.
    Ditto,   dwelling, King George street, near Old Town.
LEWIS Philip, physician, Old Town, 28, Bridge street.
LEWIS Nathaniel, taylor, dwelling, East street, between St. Pauls Lane and
Liberty streets.
LIGETTE George, dwelling, 212, Baltimore street.
LIGHTNER John, labourer, Old Town, No. Green street.
LINAHAN William, huckster, Upper Water street.
LINCK Nicholas, labourer, Pratt st. between Eutau and Paca sts.
LINDENBERGER George and Christopher, dry good store, 204, Baltimore street.
LINDENBERGER George, dwelling, 59, Beltimore street.
LINDENBERGER Charles, cabinet maker, So. side of Second street
LINHART Henry, hatter, Montgomery street, Federal Hill.
LINSY Michael, labourer, Old Town, Stigers lane
LINVILL John, comb maker, 70, Baltimore street.
LISKUY Peter, cooper, Ruxton Lane, between Light and Charles streets.
LITTLE John Miles, physician, 15, Bank street.
LITTLE Robert, rigger, Fell's Point, Apple Alley.
LITSINGBURG ---, coopers shop, 56, South street.
LIVESEY William, grocery store, 10, Pratt street.
LIVER Arnold, hatter, Dutch Alley, between Howard and Liberty streets.
    Ditto,   hatters shop, 24, So. Calvert street.
LYETH Samuel, carpenter, Dutch Alley, between Howard and Eutau streets.
LYNCH Benjamin, oysterman, Old Town, Bridge street, beyond Winon street.
LYNCH Abraha, carpenter, Old Town, Bridge street, do.
LYNCH ---, clockmaker, Boundary street.
LYNES William, taylor, 7, Bank street.
LYNN Mary, widow, Old Town, Jones street.
LYON Benjamin, furrier, 56, No. Frederic street.
LOCK Jacob, bricklayer, Alley between St. Pauls Lane and Calvert street.
LOCKS Nathaniel, grocery store, 40, So. Calvert street.
LOCKART ---, of St. Domingo, Ruxton Lane, between Light and Charles streets.
LOGAN Michael, grocer, Fell's Point, 48, Philpot street.
LOGSDON Job, cordwainer, No. side of Lexington street.

LOGUE William, carpenter, Fell's Point, Argyle Alley.
LONEY Amos, flour store, 53, light street
LONEY Hammond, carman, Fell's Point, Strawberry Alley.
LONG William, dry good store, 19, Baltimore street.
LONG Edward, grocery store, 234, Baltimore street.
LONG Robert Cary, carpenter, 8, Hanover street.
LONG Robert, dwelling,   79, No. Howard street.
LONG John, grocery store, Fell's Point, Ann street, between Pitt and Alisanna
streets.
LONG Samuel, taylor, Fell's Point, 40, Thames street.
LONG Thomas, taylor, Fell's Point, 10, Bond street.
LONG James, clark of the market, Old Town, 1, Front street.
LONG Samuel, hack carriage keeper, Old Town. Forrest street.
LONGLY Edmund, rope maker, So. Howard street.
LONGPORT George, butcher, Bank street, near Fell's Point.
LOPSTEN Andrew, baker, Fell's Point, Apple Alley.
LORMAN William, merchant, store and counting house, 14, Bowley's Wharf.
     Ditto   dwelling, 27, St. Paul's Lane.
LOUDERMAN Henry, carman, Fell's Point, 21, Alisanna street.
LOUDERMAN John, ship joiner, Fell's Point, Apple Alley.
LOVE James, oysterman, Fell's Point, 50, Wilks street.
LOW Cornelius, sea captain, Fell's Point, 99, Bond street.
LOWRY William and Co, merchants, 5, So. Calvert street.
LUBERE   confectioner, 4, Harrison street
LUCAS Francis,   Alley between Light and Charles sts.
LUDWICK Peter, inn keeper, 34, Market Place street.
LUDWIG Simon, butcher & sausage maker, 12, So. Howard st.
LUKE John,   Old Town, 28, French street.
LUPORT Martin, waggoner, Hanover street, Federal Hill.
LUTTER Thomas, book binder, Old Town, 35, Front street.
LUTZ Valentine, labourer, Lombard street.

MACK Margaret, widow, seamstress, Fell's Point, East side of Bond street,
upper end.
MACKADOO Elizabeth, washerwoman, No. Liberty street.
MACKENHEIMER John, carpenter, Old Town, 42, Bridge street.
MACKENHEIMER Peter, carpenter, Old Town, 44, do.
     Ditto   dry good store do.   42, do.
MACKIE Ebenezer, cashier of the Bank of Maryland, dwelling, South street.
MACKIE   wet goods store, Fell's Point, 28, Thames street.
MACKRILL I. surgeon and druggist, 132, Baltimore street.
MATTIER Alexander, merchant, 8, St. Pauls Lane.
MAGGS Jane, cake maker, 23, No. Gay street.
MAHONEY and JACK, flour and grocery store, 60, No. Howard st.
MALCOLM Charles, mariner, Old Town, French street, Precinct
MALHEUVRE Louis, boarding house, 41, Charles street.
MALONY John, blacksmith, Old Town, Duke street.
MAN Fight, carpenter, Old Town, No. Green street.
MAN Mary Ann, boarding house, 71, Water street.
MANGREE Samuel, shop keeper, 46, Charles street.
MANRO Jonathan, grocery store, 240, Baltimore street.
MANN Anthony, druggist, 120, Baltimore street.
MARA Robert, street paver, Fell's Point, upper end of Happy Alley.
MAREAN Jonas, merchant, store and counting house, 13, Bowley's Wharf.
MARES Jonathan, labourer, back of East street, near St. Paul's Lane.
MARCHAND Peter, mason, 19, St. Paul's Lane.

MARIN Matthew, baker, Fell's Point, 87, Bond street.
MARSH Andrew, bricklayer, Old Town, Albermarle street.
MARSH William, carpenter, 19, No. Gay street.
MARSH John, flour store, Fayette, between Liberty and Howard streets.
MARIE   , Fell's Point, 88, Bond street.
MARSHALL Sophia, widow, Old Town, Ploughman street.
MARSHALL John, inn keeper, Fell's Point, 17, Wilk's street.
MARSHALL James, retail shop, Alley between St. Paul's Lane and Calvert street.
MARSHALL John, painter and glazier, Fell's Point, Lancaster Alley, East of Bond street.
MARSTON David, smith & farrier, Fell's Point, 6, Market street.
MARTIN John, taylor, 218, Baltimore street.
MARTIN & JAUFFRET, dry good store, 59, No. Gay street.
MARTIN Luther, attorney, Gen. of Maryland, office No. Charles st.
MARTIN --- widow, 184, Baltimore street, back.
MARTIN ---, sailmaker, Fell's Point, 79, Bond street.
MARTIN Nicholas, waggoner, Old Town, Bridge street, beyond Winon street.
MARTIN Hugh, carpenter, Old Town, 27, So. High street.
MARTIN James, cabinet maker, Lovely Lane, between Calvert and South streets.
MARTIN Athenasius,   Old Town, 47, Front street.
MASS Jacob, stone mason, Old Town, Bridge street, beyond Winon street.
MASS John, cooper, Fayette street, between Howard and Eutau streets.
MASON George, grocer, 42, No. Howard street.
MASON Richard, mariner, Fell's Point, Strawberry Alley.
MASON Richard, cordwainer, Fell's Point, Argyle Alley.
MASSY Joseph, merchant, dwelling, 101, Hanover street.
     Ditto   store and countin house, 89, South street, Bowley's Wharf.
MATCHETT George, school room, 19, Bank street.
MATELIN Anthony, cutler, 26, Light street.
MATHEWS William, merchant, store and counting house, 50, So. Calvert street.
     Ditto   dwelling, 7, Water street.
     Ditto   warehouse, Mc'Clures Wharf.
MATHEWS William P. druggist, 117, Baltimore street.
MATHEWS William P., dwelling, 13, St. Paul's Lane.
MATHEWS Patrick, boarding house, Fell's Point, So. side Queen street.
MATHEWS Ann, bran and meal store, Old Town, 17, So. High street.
MATHEW Christian, taylor, Little York street, near the Wind Mill.
MATNEY Henry, cordwainer, 47, No. Gay street.
MATTISON Aaron, hatter's shop, East street, between Calvert and Gay streets.
     Ditto   dwelling, 16, No. Gay street.
MATTSON James, baker and inn keeper, Fell's Point, 21, Fell's st.
MAWRY Mary, widow, seamstress, Alley between Light and Charles streets.
MAXWELL Jemima, widow, seamstress, So. side of Camdon street.
MAY & PAYSON, merchants, store and counting house, 75, South street, Bowley's Wharf.
MAY William, pilot, Fell's Point, 6, Shakespear's Alley.
MAYERS Christian, merchant, dwelling, So. side of Camdon st.
M'ALLISTER james,   , Public Alley
M'BRIDE Mary, widow, Fell's Point, 8, Thames street.
M'CABE Thomas, cabinet maker, 34, Water street.
     Ditto   dwelling, Old Town, 88, So. High street.
M'CABE Rebecca, widow, seamstress and nurse, back of East street, near St. Paul's Lane.
M'CALLISTER John, drayman, Old Town, No. Winon street.
M'CALLISTER Bridget, boarding house, Bank street, between Light and Charles streets.

M'CALLUN & CLINE, blacksmiths, Fell's Point, 33, George street.
M'CAMON Joseph, ship chandler and dry good store, 53, South street.
M'CANN John, mariner, Fell's Point, Argyle Alley.
M'CANNON James, taylor 129, Baltimore streets.
M'CARTER Sarah, grocery store, 28, Light street.
M'CARTER Dobbin, drayman, 22, Pratt street.
M'CASKY Samuel, labourer, 40, Light street.
M'CASKEY Alexander, dry good store, Fell's Point, 1, Market street.
M'CAUSLAND Marcus, merchant, dwelling, 16, So. Calvert street.
----Ditto   grocery store,   3, Water street.
--- Ditto   warehouse,   M'Clures Wharf.
--- Ditto   soap and candle factory, 10, Bank street.
M'CLARTY John, blacksmith, Fell's Point, 10, Shakespears Alley
MCCLEEN Thomas, taylor, Montgomery street, Federal Hill.
MCCONNEL William, carpenter, 35, No. Gay street.
MCCONKEY William, carpenter, Old Town, Granby street.
MCCORMICK James & Co. merchants, 236, Baltimore street.
--- Ditto   dwelling, 32, South street.
MCCORMICK & De BUTTS, hardware store, 7, So. Calvert street.
MCCOY Andrew, wool card maker, 83, Nor. Howard street.
MCCOY Mathew, labourer, Waggon Alley, between Howard and Eutau streets.
MCCOY John, dry good store, Fell's Point, 19, Fell's street.
MCCREERY William, merchant, 9, So. Calvert street.
MCCULLOCK & BIRKHEAD, Merchants, store and counting house, 87, Southstreet,
Bowley's Wharf.
MCCALLOUGH James H. merchant, dwelling, 8, Commerce street.
MCCURLY Hugh, merchant, 16, So. Calvert street.
--- Ditto   dwelling, 109 Baltimore street.
MCDERMOT Grace, widow, seamstress, Bank street, near Fell's Point.
MCDERMOT Thomas, labourer, Fell's Point, 62, Bond street.
MCDONALD Alexander, inn keeper, Fell's Point, 62, Bond street.
MCDONALD William, grocery store, Fell's Point, 7, Market st.
MCDONELL John, drayman, 21 No. Gay street.
MCDONNELL Barnet, mason, Conowago street.
MCDONNEL Samuel, cordwainer, Fell's Point, 21 Bond street.
MCDONNOUGH & BAXLEY, dry good store, 168 Baltimore street.
MCDOWALL Thomas, tallow chandler, Fell's Point, 31, Wilk's st.
MCDOWALL George, bookseller and stationer, 3 South street.
MCELDERY Thomas, dwelling, Old Town, near friends meeting house.
--- Ditto   soap and candle factory, 15, Commerce street.
MCELHINEY George, dry good store, 46, Baltimore street.
MCELROY James, drayman, Saratoga street.
MCFADON Rebecca, widow, boarding house, 37, So. Calvert st.
MCFADON John & Co. merchants, store and counting house, 5 Bowley's Wharf.
--- Ditto   dwelling Old Town, Granby street.
MCFADON William & Co. lumber yard, McClures Wharf.
MCFADON William, merchant, dwelling Old Town, Ploughmans street.
MCFARLAND Michael, carpenter, 60 No. Frederic street.
MCGILTON Daniel, cordwainer, 4, Light street.
MCGLUSHIN William, plaisterer, Primrose Alley, between Light and Charles sts.
MCGONGIN Daniel, cordwainer, Conowago street.
MCGOWEN John,   Old Town, Albermarle street.
MCGUIRE Roger, labourer, Old Town, Albermarle street.
MCGUIRE Thomas, dry good store, Fell's Point, 15, George st.
MCHENRY Francis, grocery store, 15 Cheapside.

MCHENRY Dennis, cordwainer and Inn keeper, 17 Conowago st.
MCILVAIN Alexander, taylor, 42 So. Calvert street.
MCINTIRE Patrick, grocer, 20 Pratt street.
MCKEAN John, dwelling McClelens Alley.
---- Ditto & Co. china and glass store, 224, Baltimore street.
MCKEE Thomas, clark, passage back of St. Paul's Lane.
MCKENNA Francis, grocery store, 184 Baltimore street.
MCKENNY   , drayman, German street, between Howard and Eutau streets.
MCKENZIE Benjamin, inn keeper, Fell's Point, 14 Shakespear's Alley.
MCKENZIE Mary, widow, Old Town, So. Green street.
MCKENZIE William, cooper, Old Town, Front street, adjoining English Church.
MCKERNAN Michael, grocer, Fell's Point, 54, Bond street.
MCKIM Samuel, dry good store, 47 Baltimore street.
MCKIM John, junr. Merchant, 56 Baltimore street.
MCKIM John, merchant, 78 Baltimore street.
MCKIM Robert, dry good store, 103 Baltimore street.
MCKIM Robert & Alexander, merchants, 14 South street.
MCKINLY Neale, drayman, Conowago street.
MCKINNEL   , cordwainer, Conowago street.
MCKINNEY Roderic, rope maker, Fell's Point, 11 Fleet street.
MCKINSEY William, coopers shop, 54 South street.
MCKNIGHT & FINLEY, grocery store, 22 No. Howard street.
MCKNIGHT David, dwelling Fayette street, between Liberty and Howard streets.
MCKOY John, hair dresser and perfumer, 185 Baltimore street.
MCMECHEN David, attorney at law, 4 No. Calvert street.
MCMECHEN William, cordwainer, Fell's Point, 47 Wilk's st.
MCMULLEN Robert, labourer, Lombard street.
MCMYERS John, block maker, Fell's Point, 46 Philpot street.
MCNEMARA Thomas, cordwainer, Fell's Point, 51 Wilk's st.
MCPHERSON William, labourer, Barre street. Federal Hill.
MEAD Phebe, washerwoman, Cow-pen Lane.
MEADWELL James, Innkeeper, 18 Market place.
MEADWELL Alexander, waggoner, Forrest street, Federal Hill.
MEDCALF Abraham, butcher, Fell's Point, 1 George street.
MEFFORD John, cordwainer, Waggon Alley, between Howard and Eutau streets.
MEGAN Margaret, widow, No. Charles street.
MEGY Madam, grocer, Fell's Point, 100 Bond street.
MENELLI John, drayman, Old Town, North street.
MENTA John Peter, cutler, 2 Harrison street.
MERCER Benjamin James, constable and inn keeper, 34 Light st.
MEROSSY Joseph, mason, 27 No. Gay street.
MERRICKEN Charles, wood corder, North side, Lexington street.
MERRYMAN John, dwelling 4 so. Calvert street.
MERRYMAN Benjamin & J. dwelling Old Town, 5 Bridge street.
    Ditto   dry good store, Old Town, 7 Bridge street.
MESSERSMITH & BARRY, dry and wet good store, 51 No. GRy st.
    Ditto   ditto, Old Town, 47 Bridge street.
MESSERSMITH Samuel, dwelling 53 No. Gay street.
MESSONNIER Henry, merchant, dwelling, 45 South street.
    Ditto   store and counting house, 69 South street, Bowley's Wharf.
METEREAU Jacques, labourer, Fell's Point, 15 Philpot street.
METZLER Daniel, cordwainer, 32 No. Frederic street.
MICKLE John, street commissioner, East street - between St. Pauls Lane and
No. Charles street.
MILES Daniel, mariner, Fell's Point, Wolf street.
MILTZ William, plaisterer, Old Town, Duke street.

MILLER Anthony, musician, Old Town, Granby street.
MILLER Peter, tobacconist, 27 South street.
MILLER William, inn keeper & boarding house, 1 No. Calvert st.
MILLER John, baker & inn keeper, 94 Charles street.
MILLER John, dwelling 77 No. Howard street.
MILLER Mathias, shop keeper, South side of Camdon street.
MILLER Margaret, widow, cake shop, East street - between Calvert and Gay sts.
MILLER Adam, butcher, Fayette - between Howard and Eutau streets.
MILLER Christian, distiller, North side Lexington street.
MILLER Henry, carpenter, Saratoga street.
MILLER Frederic, --- Eutau street.
MILLER John, windsor chair maker, Waggon Alley -- between Howard and Liberty
streets
MILLER John, inn keeper, Fell's Point, 71 Bond street.
MILLER Frederic, drayman, Old Town, No. Green street.
MILLER Jacob, tanyard, Old Town, Bridge street.
MILLER John, hack carriage keeper, Old Town, 8 Bridge street.
MILLER George, blacksmith, Old Town, York street.
MILLER James, coach maker, Second street - near the Falls.
MILLER Jacob, inn keeper, Paca street.
MILLER Elizabeth, widow, 24 No. Frederic street.
MILLETS George, baker, Dutch Alley - between Howard and Liberty streets.
MILLION Patrick biscuit baker, 72 South street, Bowley's Wharf.
MILLNER Frederic, taylor, 36 So. Calvert street.
MILTENBERGHER George, leather dresser, 4 Market Place.
MINCHIN J. wine store, 24 Water street.
MINE Marcus, carman, Old Town, Stiger Lane.
MINGO John carpenter, 8 No. Liberty street.
MINIC Baltzer, cordwainer, 48 No. Howard street.
MINTS Joseph, drayman, Bank street - near Fell's Point.
MINOT & NEWHALL, boot and shoe factory, 173 Baltimore street.
MIRANDE Mathew, dry good store, 16, Baltimore street.
MISSING Christian, phycisian, 2 Baltimore street.
MITCHELL Francis, dry good store, 51 Baltimore street.
MITCHELL & SHEPPARD, grocery store, 20 Cheapside.
MITCHELL Peter, cooks shop, 6 Market Place.
MITCHELL John, dwelling, 74, Pratt street.
MITCHEL Charles, bricklayer, Forrest Lane.
MITCHELL John, pilot, Fell's Point, 42, Market street.
MITCHEL Arthur, cooper, Old Town, 31, French street.
MYERS Jacob, china store, 55, Baltimore street.
MYERS Jacob, tobacconist, 55, South street.
MYERS Charles, dry good store, 1, So. Gay street.
MYERS William, flour and grocery store, 44, No. Howard street.
MYERS Jeremiah, labourer, North street, Log Town.
MYER Hannah, widow, washerwoman, Fell's Point, Lancaster Alley, East of Bond
street.
MYERS Nicholas, mariner, Fell's Point, 6, Shakespear's Alley.
MYERS Christian, dwelling, Old Town, 30, Bridge street.
   Ditto   dry good store, do. 32,   do.
MYER Philip, baker, Old Town, No. Winon street.
MYERS John, cordwainer, Old Town, 29, French street.
MYERS Margaret, widow, Old Town, York street.
MYERS Jacob, baker, Conway street, Federal Hill.
MYERS Robert, ship carpenter, Brioy Alley, Federal Hill.

MYLES Zachary, grocery store, 228, Baltimore street.
MOALE Richard, attorney at law, Lovely Lane, between Calvert and South stts.
MOALE Thomas, hardware store, 21, So. Calvert street.
MOALE John, dwelling, German street, between Hanover and Liberty streets.
MOCKBEE William, hatter, East street, between St. Paul Lane and Charles st.
MOELLINGER Frederic, schoolmaster, Old Town, North street.
MOFFITT John, grocery store, 6, County Wharf.
MOISSONNIER Francis, late French Consul, 17, So. Gay street.
MOLAR David, butcher, 57, No. Howard street.
MOLIER Henry and Co. grocery and commission store, 26 South st.
MONBUISSON DeBas, widow, of St. Domingo, 64, Pratt street.
MONCRIEFF Archibald, merchant, dwelling and counting house, 14, Water street.
MONDAY John, grocery store, 58, No. Gay street.
MONDEL William, carpenter, Fell's Point, west side of Bond street, upper end.
MONROE Peter, copper plate painter, Old Town, Bridge street, beyond Winon st.
MONTALIBAU of St. Domingo, Old Town, Jones street.
MONTGOMERY Joseph, drayman, Lovely Lane, between Calvert and South streets.
MOOCHEL Samuel, butcher, Old Town, No. Green street.
MOORE William S. dry good store, 64, Baltimore street.
MOORE Philip, clark of district court of Maryland, dwelling, 54, No. Gay st.
MOORE William, flour store, 77, No. Howard street.
MOORE John, carpenter, Hill street Federal Hill.
MOORE Daniel, Inspector of flour, north side of Camdon street.
MOORE Henry, painter and glazier, Fayette between Howard and Eutau streets.
MOORE John, Mariner, Fell's Point, east side of Bond street - upper end.
MOORE Thomas, sea captain, Fell's Point, 16 Wilk's street.
MOORE Jane, widow, Exeter street - near the Wind Mill.
MOORE William, carman, Ruxton lane, between Light and Charles streets.
MOORE Jacob, painter and glazier, Paca street.
MOORES Daniel, physician, 17 Baltimore street.
MORANGE Peter Paul, merchant of St. Domingo, Gough street, near Fell's Point.
MORANGE Etienne, miniature Portrait painter, Lee street - Fed. Hill.
MOREL Lewis -- of St. Domingo, Barre street - Fed. Hill.
MORELLIE Gaspar, hatter, 36 Charles street.
MORETON John, butcher, Old Town, Duke street.
MORETON John, cabinet maker, Lemmon's alley
MORRETTE --- of St. Domingo, Saratoga street.
MORGAN Jesse, grocery store, 253 Baltimore street.
MORGAN Robert, boatman, Lombard street.
MORGAN William, rigger, Fell's Point, Apple alley.
MORGAN Thomas, inn-keeper, Fell's Point, 28 Fell's street.
MORGAN Thomas, cooper, Old Town, 33 Front street.
MORGAN Thomas, Potter, Old Town, south Green street.
MORIN Pierre, jeweller of St. Domingo, 47 North Howard st.
MORSE Abraham, innkeeper, Fell's Point, Lancaster alley.
MORSEL Benjamin, carpenter, Fell's Point, Ann street.
MORTIMER Thomas, mariner, north side of Camdon street.
MORRA Thomas, butcher, Second street - between Gay street and the Falls.
MORRIS William, innkeeper, Old Town, Bridge street - beyond Winon street.
MORRISON James, painter and glazier, 9 Bank street.
MORRISON John, cordwainer, south Frederic street.
MORROW John, soap and tallow chandler, 46 Market place.
MORRY Joseph, codrwainer, Bank street - near Fell's Point.
MOSHER James, bricklayer, 15 St. Paul's lane.
MOSIER Philip, blacksmith, Old Town, Albermarle street.

MONCHET Henry -- of St. Domingo, Fell's Point, south side of Fleet street.
MOULE Joseph and James, dry goods store, 33 So. Calvert st.
--- Ditto, dwelling, 128 Baltimore street.
MOULE Thomas, dwelling, 18 Light street.
MOULLINS Jean Baptiste, milliner's shop, 36 north Gay street.
MOURIES Joseph, waterman, Fell's Point, Apple alley.
MULENIER Claude, hair dresser, upper Water street.
MULL Jacob, Turner's Shop, Fell's Point, south side of Queen st.
MULLAN Patrick, dry good store, Old Town, 31 Bridge street.
MUNDAY William, Store keeper, 63 north Howard street.
MUNIER Claude Louis, boarding house, 11 Gay street.
MUNNICKHUYSEN and SADDLER, merchants, store and counting house, 65 South street, Bowley's Wharf.
MURS Joseph, soap and tallow chandler, Fell's Point, 39 Bond street, Back.
MURPHY William, taylor, 65 Baltimore street.
MURPHY John, grocery store, 145 Baltimore street.
MURPHY Patrick, taylor and inn keeper, 29 Light street.
MURPHY James, blacksmith, Fell's Point, 51 Bond street, Back.
MURPHY John, sea captain, Fell's Point, No. side of Fleet street.
MURPHY James, inn keeper, Hanover street, Federal Hill.
MURPHY Mary, widow, seamstress, Alley between Light and Charles streets.
MURRAY James, painter and Glazier, Old Town, Low street.
MUSKY Catherine, huckster, Fell's Point, 39 Wilk's street.
MUSSBERGHER David, carpenter, Eutau street.

NACE George, dwelling 28 No. Howard street.
NADACE John,   , Sharp street.
NASH Charles, carpenter, Brioy Alley, Federal Hill.
NASH Thomas, carpenter, Fell's Point, Argyle Alley.
NEALE Edward and Co. dry good store, 207, Baltimore street.
NEALE John B. dry good store, 22 So. Calvert street.
NEALE John, coach maker, 17 No. Gay street.
NEAL Hugh, sexton to Presbyterian Church, So. side of Lexington street.
NEAL John, labourer, Fell's Point, Argyle Alley.
NEAL Samuel, gardiner, Old Town, 79 So. High street.
NEAMAN Jacob, coopers shop and grocery store, 229, Baltimore street.
NEIGHBOURS Henry, ship carpenter, Fell's Point, Alisanna street.
NELSON Thomas, sea captain, Fell's Point, 102 Bond street.
NELSON Robert, merchant, Old Town, So. Green street.
NELSON Valentine, carman, Cyder Alley.
NESBIT William, rope dancer, Waggon Alley - between Howard and Liberty streets.
NEWCOMER John, butcher, Dutch Alley - between Howard and Liberty streets.
NEWSON George, carpenter, Sharp street.
NEWTON William, constable and tavern keeper, 87 Hanover street.
NICOLS James, merchant, 246 Baltimore street.
NICOLS Haskins and Co. merchants, store and counting house, 7 Bowley's Wharf.
NICOLS Henry, dwelling, East street - between Calvert & Gay sts.
NICOLL Warrell Lysle, merchant, Fell's Point, 11 Thames street.
NICHOLSON John Powell, store keeper, Old Town, Bridge street - beyond Winon st.
NICHOLSON John, merchant, dwelling, 9 St. Paul's Lane.
NIEUMAN Jacob, cooper, German street - between Howard and Liberty streets.
NIPPARD John, sausage maker, Old Town, 79 So. High street.
NIPPARD George, sausage maker, Old Town, Temple street.
NOGLE Peter, taylor, Triplet's Alley.
NOLAN William, cordwainer, 50 No. Gay street.

NORQUAY Magnus, retail shop, 25 Cheap side.
NORRIS Benjamin, tavern and boarding house, Fell's Point, 41 Bond street.
NORRIS James, inn keeper and hay weigher, Old Town, North street.
NORRIS Abraham, labourer, Old Town, North street.
NOUVEL Peter,   of St. Domingo, Fell's Point, Apple Alley.
NOWLAN William, ship carpenter, Fell's Point, 24 George street.
NOWLAND Peregrine, inn keeper, 219 Baltimore street.
NOWLAND Peter, hiar dresser, 205 Baltimore street.
NURSER Sebastian, retail shop, Fayette street - between Howard and Eutau sts.
NUSSEER Jacob, cordwainer, West side of North Liberty street.
NUTTER William, labourer, Fell's Point, Apple Alley

OATES William, barbar, Fell's Point, 8 Bond street.
OATELSTON Joseph, stone cutter, Old Town, 21 Front street.
OBLANE John, inn keeper, Fell's Point, 17 Fell's streets.
O'BRIAN Charles, dwelling, 1 Bank street.
    Ditto   grocery store, 26 So. Calvert street.
O'BRIEN Joseph D. grocery store, Fell's Point, 1 Pitt street.
O'BRYAN Michael, carpenter, Fayette - between Liberty and Howard streets.
OCCAMON George, caulker, Fell's Point, Ann street.
ODOIN Julia, widow, Primrose Alley - between Light and Charles streets.
OFFORT Charles, mariner, alley between Light and Charles streets.
OGE Jean Louis, of St. Domingo, 2 North Liberty streets.
OGLE George, drayman, Fell's Point, Pitt street.
OBLEBY & WHINCHESTER, merchants, store and counting house, South street,
Bowley's Wharf.
O'HARA Samuel, painter and glazier, 19 South Gay street.
OLDHAM John, windsor chair maker, 43, South street.
OLIVE Jean Baptiste, grocery store, 252, Baltimore street.
OLIVER Robert, merchant, dwelling 22, So. Gay street.
OLIVER and THOMPSON, merchants, counting house, 25, Second st.
OLIVIER Francois, of St. Domingo, Old Town, Jones's street.
OTONIER Delisle, dwelling, 21, Commerce street.
O'NEAL Bernard, inn keeper, Fell's Point, 16, Thames street.
ORCHARD Thomas, cordwainer, Old Town, 15 French street.
O'ROURKE Patrick, of St. Domingo, 45 Pratt street.
ORT Matthew, shingle dresser, 96, Pratt street.
ORRICK Rebecca, widow, Forrest street, Federal Hill.
OSBORN Joseph, carpenter, passage between Waggon Alley and Fayette street.
OSBORNE Jonas, inn keeper, Fell's Point, to Fell's street.
OSBORNE John, cordwainer, Fell's Point 12 Fell's street.
OSBORN John, labourer, Old Town, No. Winon street.
OSBORNE Samuel So. side of Bank street, between Light and Charles streets.
OSBORNE Eleanor, widow, Primrose Alley, between Light and Charles streets.
OSBORNE Robert, dry good store, 54 Market Place.
OSBORNE Robert, dry good store, 44 Market Place.
OSFORD, Frances, seamstress, Fell's Point, 41 Wilks's street.
OTTO Anthony, inn keeper, 8 Market Place.
OTTER Henry, labourer, Paca street.
OTTERBINE William, clergyman, Conway street, Federal Hill.
OVAL Elizabeth, washerwoman, Fell's Point, 32 Queen street.
OVERULSER John, cordwainer, Dutch Alley, between Howard and Liberty streets.
OWENS William, dry good store, 113 Baltimore street.
OWINGS Samuel, merchant, dwelling, 65 Hanover street.
OWRAM Mary, widow, seamstress, Fell's Point, 19 Fleet street.

PAGE John, cordwainer, Old Town, Stiger Lane.
PAILLOTTET Joseph, teacher of French, Primrose Alley, between Light and Charles streets.
PALLON James, boarding house, 2 So. Gay street.
PAMPHILION Thomas, Fell's Point, 14 Bond street.
PANNELL Edward, grocery store, 33 South street.
PANNELLS John, dwelling, Fell's Point, 21 Philpot street.
    Ditto,   ship chandler's store, do. 23 do.
PARKER Robert, cooper's shop, 58 South street.
PARKER John, bricklayer, Eutau street.
PARKER James, sea captain, Fell's Point, 21 Shakespear's Alley.
PARKER John, Pilot, Sharp street.
PARKS John, hatter's shop, 14 Light street.
    Ditto dwelling, 137 Baltimore street.
PARKS Nathan, carman, Eden street. - near Fell's Point.
PARKS John.   do.   do.   do.
PARKS Archibald, carman, Bank street - near Fell's Point.
PARKS William, shop keeper. do.   do.
PARKS Frederic, carman,   do.   do.
PARKS John, drayman, Gough street,   do.
PARRIAN Joseph, gardiner, Old Town, Pitt street.
PARSONS Daniel, taylor, Waggon Alley - between Howard and Liberty streets.
PARSONS John, taylor, Lee street, Federal Hill.
PARSONS William, ship carpenter, Hanover street. - Federal Hill.

PASEAULT Louis P. merchant, dwelling 237 Baltimore street.
    Ditto   store and counting house, 4 So. Gay street.
PATTERSON William, merchant, president of the Bank of Maryland, 18 South st.
    Ditto   warehouse Mc'Clures Wharf
PATTERSON Samuel, drayman, Conowago street.
PATTERSON James, taylor, Fell's Point, 36 Thames street.
PATTERSON William, cabinet maker, Old Town, Albermarle st.
PATTERSON   , mariner, Fell's Point, 26, Wilk's street.
PATRIDGE William, bricklayer, 17 St. Paul's Lane.
PAUL Augustin,   of St. Domingo, Old Town, So. Green st.
PAULSON Matthew, sea captain, East street - between St. Paul's Lane and Liberty streets.
PAYSON Henry, dwelling, 54 Hanover street.
PEACHEY William T. hardware store, 138 Baltimore street.
PEARCE Richard, dry good store, 10 So. Calvert street.
PEACOCK John, cordwainer, Eutau street.
PEAS   , sea captain, Conway street, Federal Hill.
PECHIN William, printer, office 15 Baltimore street.
PECK Francis, carman, So. Frederic street.
PECK Nathaniel, grocery store, 191 Baltimore street.
PEIRCE Humphrey, merchant, 95 Baltimore street.
PIERCE Israel, dry good store, 109 Baltimore street.
    Ditto   dwelling, Lovely Lane - between Calvert and South streets.
PEIR James, ---, Mongomery street, Federal Hill.
PEEL William, ship joiner, 84 Charles street.
PEEL George, bricklayer, West side of No. Liberty street.
PELL William, labourer, No. side of Camdon street.
PENNINGTON Henry, bricklayer, Old Town, So. Green street.
PERIER Pierre, taylor, 158 Baltimore street.
PERINE Maulden, potter, Old Town, Queen street.
PERINE Simon, bricklayer, Bottle Alley, between Howard and Eutau streets, So. of Baltimore street.

PERUSE   , taylor, 13 No. Gay street.
PERRIGO Joseph, bricklayer, Old Town, 25, Front street.
PERRY Richard, labourer, 21 So. Howard street.
PERRYMAN Isaac, bricklayer, New Church street.
PETER John, shop keeper, King George street - Old Town.
PETERS, JOHNSTON & Co. brewery, King George street, Old Town.
PETERS Daniel, tinman, 4 So. Frederic street.
PETERS Michael, blacksmith, Old Town, Duke street.
PETERS Dolly, widow,   So. Howard street.
PETERS Henry,   , 116, No. Howard street.
PETERS George   dwelling, 31 No. Howard street.
PETERS Conrad, bricklayer, 117 No. Howard street.
PETERSON Joseph, pedler, Eden street - near Fell's Point.
PETERSON Martha, widow, seamstress - back of East street.
PHELAN John, school room, Alley between St. Paul's Lane and No. Calvert st.
PHILE Charles, inn keeper, Conowago street.
PHILIP   , measurer of Grain, Saratoga street.
PHILIP Etienne, caulker, King George street - near Fell's Point.
PHILIPS Bethia, widow, boarding house, 11 Bank street.
PHILIPPE & LE GRAS, jewellers, clock and watch makers, 156 Baltimore streets.
PHILPOT Brian, dwelling Old Town, York street.
PHOLOCH   , Old Town, 27 Front street.
PICKHAVEN Jonathan, plaisterer, Waggon Alley - between Howard and Eutau sts.
PIERCE Thomas, sea captain and inn keeper, Fell's Point, 5 Fell's street.
PIERSON Mary, widow, washerwoman, No. side of Lexington st.
PIERPOINT Joseph, grocery store, 33 Light street.
PIERPOINT John, blacksmith, 25 So. Howard street.
PIERPOINT Thomas, carpenter, 17 St. Paul's Lane.
PIFER   , labourer, Lombsrd street.
PIKE James, pilot, Fell's Point, 6 Shakespear's Alley.
PILCH James, rigger, Fell's Point - West side of Bond street, - upper end.
PILGRIM Joseph, fruit shop, 20 1/2 So. Calvert street.
PINDLE John Larkin, coach maker, Old Town, 72 So. High st.
PINFIELD Nancy, seamstress and washerwoman, north Liberty st.
PINTZEL John, carpenter, 21 Second street.
PINTZEL Baltzer, carpenter and joiner, 5 So. Gay street.
PIPER James, dwelling, 108 Hanover street.
PIPER James, grocery store, 40 No. Howard street.
PITT Thomas, labourer, So. side of Lexington street.
PITT William, pilot, Fell's Point, 44 Philpot streets.
PYE Eleanor, seamstress, Fell's Point, Argyle Alley.
PLASTER Mordecai, clerk, No. Charles street.
PLEASANTS &\Co. merchants, 197, Baltimore street.
PLEICHROTH George Henry, baker, Fell's Point, 11 Alisanna st.
PLOCH Andrew, painter, Old Town, Forrest street.
PLUNKETT   , widow, So. Frederic street.
POE David, dry good store, 173 Baltimore street.
POE George, shoe factory, 183 Baltimore street.
POE Jane, widow, German street - between Hanover street and Howard streets.
POINTS James, cooper, No. Lexington street.
POIRIER Peter,   , 42 Charles street.
POLK Charles P. dry good store, 35 So. Calvert street.
POLLOCK Susannah, widow, huskster, 9 South street.
POLLOCK Elias, black ball maker, Old Town, 13 Front street.
     Ditto   toy shop, Old Town, 12 Bridge street.
POLY Jacob, plaisterer, Old Town, 86 So. High street.

PONS Anthony, inn keeper, Fell's Point, 48 Thames street.
PONTIER Anthony, perfumer and hiar dresser, 34 South street.
POOLS Joseph, comb maker, Triplets Alley.
POPPE John, hair dresser, Waggon Alley – between Howard and Eutau streets.
PORTER David, sea captain, Montgomery street – Federal Hill.
POSE Daniel, blacksmith, Fell's Point, 24 Fell's street.
POTAN   , 30 No. Frederic street.
POULTNEY Thomas, hardware store, 162 Baltimore street.
POUPONNEAU Olivier, joiner, 60 Charles street.
POWERS James, bricklayer, 15 Pratt street.
POWTHER Leonard, carpenter, 68 No. Howard street.
PRAT Pierce, grocery store, 56 Charles street.
PRATT Frederic, dry good store, 107 Baltimore street.
PRATT James, rigger, Fell's Point, West side of Bond street – upper end.
PRATTENS Caroline, widow, dry good store, 141 Baltimore street.
PRENTICE Alexander, taylor, East – between Calvert and Gay sts.
PRESBURY George Goldsmith, justice of the peace, 38 North Gay street.
PRESBURY Joseph, schoolmaster, Fell's Point, 5 Wilk's street.
PRESTON William, grocery store, 173 Baltimore street.
PRICE James, merchant, store and counting house, 84 South Bowley's Wharf.
   Ditto   dwelling, 96 Hanover street.
PRICE & ROBERTSON, taylors, 32 No. Gay street.
PRICE William, bricklayer and plaisterer, 99 No. Howard street.
PRICE Daniel, hack carriage driver, Saratoga street.
PRICE William, ship wright, Fell's Point, 13 Pitt street.
   Ditto   do.   14   do.
PRICE Warrick, cabinet maker, Old Town, So. High street.
PRICE Nicholas, attorney at law, Old Town, Jones street.
PRIEST Henry, schoolmaster, 68 Hanover street.
PRIESTLY Thomas, grocery store, 2 County Wharf.
PRILL Frederic, baker, 7 So. Gay street.
PRINCE John, carpenter, Old Town, 39 Front street.
PRITCHARD William, mariner, Fell's point, 5 Fleet street.
PROSSER John, butcher, Old Town, 51 So. High street.
PROVINCS Charles, mariner, Goodman street, Federal Hill
PROVOST Julien,   of St. Domingo, Old Town, French street, Precinct.
PUGH Joseph, carpenter, Dutch Alley – between Howard and Liberty streets.
PULPHREY Frederic, carpenter, So. Liberty street.
PURDONS William, carpenter, Eden street – near Fell's Point.
PURSE Thomas, watch and clock maker, 3 South street.
PURVIANCE Robert, collector for the port of Baltimore, dwelling 52 Water st.
PURVIANCE John, office, South side, Second street.

QUIN Jennet, widow, Old Town, Bridge street – beyond Winon street.
QUISICK John, carpenter, Triplet's Alley.
QUAIL Robert, cooper, Public Alley.

RABORG & DOUDLE, grocery store, 176 Baltimore street.
RABORG Christopher, copper smith and tinman, 11 Water street.
RACINE Daniel, watch maker, 74 Charles street.
RAINSFORD Elizabeth, widow, gorcery store and boarding house, 42 Light street.
RAMSAY Robert, grocery store, Fell's Point, 19 Thames street.
RAMSAY Nathaniel, Naval officer, for the port of Baltimore, 248 Baltimore st.
RAMSEY George, ship carpenter, Fell's Point, 36 Bond street.
RANDALL Samuel, cordwainer, 27 South street.
RANDALL Roger, cooper, 33 Light street.
RANDLE Rebecca & Susannah, seamstresses, So. Liberty street.

RANDAL Margaret, baker, Fell's Point, 53 Bond street.
RAPHAEL Solomon, inn keeper, Old Town, 4 Bridge street.
RATIEN & KONECKE, merchants, 154 Baltimore street.
RATREE John, taylor, Fell's Point, Apple Alley.
RAVEL Thomas, ship joiner, Fell's Point, Alisanna street.
RAWLINS Ann, mantua maker, Fell's Point, 22 Queen street.
RAYMAN Thomas, mariner, Fell's Point, 111 Bond street.
REA George, cooper, 30 Charles street.
READ James, labourer, Old Town, Pitt street.
READLE John, bottling cellar, Fell's Point, 2 Fell's street.
    Ditto   do.   7 No. Frederic street.
READAN Ruth, mantua maker, Old Town, Front street.
REDELMOSER Michael, dwelling, 238 Baltimore street.
REDON   , of St. Domingo 47 Pratt street.
REED Nelson, clergyman, 8 Light street.
REED James, sea captain, Fell's Point, 2 Queen street.
REESE John E. dwelling, 43 Charles street.
REESE Adam, carman, Fell's Point, 23 Alisanna street.
REESE Henry, cordwainer, Fell's Point, 4 Market street.
REESE Jacob, pilot, Fell's Point, Ann street.
REES & MATHEWS, curriers, 13 Water street.
REEVES Robert, mariner, Fell's Point, Lancaster Alley.
REEVES William, sea captain, Fell's Point, Ann Street.
RHABB Dutrick, shop keeper, Fell's Point, 21 Fell's street.
RHERBACK George, carpenter, 50 No. Liberty street.
RHINEHART Philip, carpenter, 100 Pratt street.
RHONEY Dennis, labourer, No. Charles street.
REID John Gillis, dry good store, 8 Baltimore street.
REID Hannah, widow, seamstress, Ruxton Lane, - between Light and Charles sts.
REID   , mariner, Eutau street.
REIFKUYEL Christian, tobacconist, 4 Baltimore street.
REIFF John, sausage maker, Eutau street.
REILY Stephen, Old Town, Wapping street.
REIN George, cordwainer, 51 South street.
REINICKER George, gorcery store 223 Baltimore street.
REITICKER Adam, carman, Gough street - near Fell's Point.
RENDAVIL Garret, inn keeper, Fell's Point, 20 Thames, street.
RENAUD Melan, of St. Domingo, Waggon Alley - West of Howard street.
RENSHAW Hannah, widow, boarding house, 12 So. Gay street.
REPOLD George, merchant, 170 Baltimore street.
REPP John, grocery store, 63 Baltimore street.
RESCANIER Peter, of St. Domingo, Fayette - between Liberty and Howard streets.
REENS Anthony, pilot, Fell's Point, 6 Pitt street.
REYNOLDS Joshua, carman, Fell's Point, Lancaster Alley.
REYNOLDS William, grocery store, 214 Baltimore street.
RICE J . and Co. bookseller, 87 Baltimore street.
RICE Joseph, watch maker, 122, Baltimore street.
RICE Eleanor, widow, Old Town, North street.
RICHARD Joseph, of St. Domingo, Alley between Light and Charles streets.
RICHARDS Lewis, clergyman, Old Town, Wapping street.
RICHARDS Edward, rigger, Fell's Point, 58 Bond street.
RICHARDS Elias, labourer, 85 Hanover street.
RICHARDSON Robert R. dry good store, 3 south Calvert street.
RICHARDSON Robert, physician, 46 Light street.
RICHARDSON Enoch, carpenter, 63 Harrison street.

RICKETTS ---, widow, No. side of Cambden street.
RICKETTS Hugh, nailer, south Liberty street.
RIDDLE John, Fell's Point, 11 Pitt street.
RIDDLE Robert, merchant, 92 Baltimore street.
RIDDLE William, carpenter, 38 Pratt street.
RIDGELY Rebecca, boarding house, 9 No. Gay street.
RIDGELY Rebecca, widow, 52 Hanover street.
RIDGELY Charles, 11 south Frederic street.
RILEY William, cordwainer, 102 Baltimore street.
--- Ditto,   dwelling, East street, between Calvert and Gay streets.
RILEY Adam, labourer, Old Town, 11 French street.
RILEY Conrad, stone quarrier, Old Town, 49 Franch street.
RILEY George, straw cutter, Old Town, Franch street - Precincts.
RILEY Dennis, labourer, Fell's Point, Lancaster Alley.
RIMAGE Nicholas, carpenter, Old Town, 18 Franch street.
RING Brien, Carolina street, near Fell's Point.
RIPPEE David, tobacconist, Hanover street, Federal Hill.
RITCHIE William, mariner, Fell's Point, 1 Fleet street.
RITES Philip, labourer, Old Town, 10 French street.
RYAN James, carpenter, Waggon Alley, West of Howard street.
RYAN Michael, innkeeper, Fell's Point, 55 Bond street.
RYDER Benjamin, drayman, Fell's Point, 3 Fleet street.
RYLAND Richard, innkeeper, Fell's Point, 7 Market place.
RYLAND Joseph, carpenter, Waggon Alley, West of Howard street.
ROACHBROOM Lewis, ship-wright, Fell's Point, 32 Pitt street.
ROACH John, weaver, Old Town, No. Green street.
ROACH Henry, dwelling, Old Town, 5 Franch street.
ROBB William, merchant, dwelling, 9 Water street.
--- Ditto, store & counting house, 77 South st. Bowley's wharf.
ROBB John, cordwainer, south Howard street.
ROBERT James, armourer, Fell's Point, 3 Thames street.
ROBERT Joseph, labourer, Old Town, Forrest street.
ROBERTS George & sons, Irish Linnen store, 244 Baltimore st.
ROBERTS Owen, carpenter, south side of Lexington street.
ROBERTS James, labourer, south side of Lexington street.
ROBERTS Richard, hair dresser, upper Water street.
ROBBINS Roger, sea captain, Fells Point, upper end of Bond st.
ROBINSON Samuel, dry good store, 61 Baltimore street.
ROBINSON Archibald, attorney at law, 7 Charles street.
ROBINSON John, grocer, 45 No. Howard street.
ROBINSON Mary, widow, tayloress, south Howard street.
ROBINSON Elizabeth, seamstress and a washerwoman, Waggon Alley, between
Howard and Liberty streets.
ROBINSON John, Mariner, Fell's Point, Apple Alley.
ROBINSON Rachel, widow, Fell's Point, Ann street, between Pitt and Alisanna
streets.
ROBISON Ephraim, flour and grocery store, 36 No. Howard st.
--- Ditto,   ware house, 38 No. Howard street.
RODDY Patrick, bricklayer, Conowago street.
ROGERS John, blacksmith, 82 Charles street.
ROE Walter, merchant, 57 Baltimore street.
ROGERS Nicholas, dwelling, 153 Baltimore street.
ROGERS Jacob, hatter, 29 South street.
ROGERS John, sea captain, Fell's Point, 15 Pitt street.
ROGERS Guy, mariner, Primrose Alley, between Light and Charles streets.

ROGERS William, flour merchant, 55 Water street.
RHODES Thomas, proprietor of the Annapolis stage, German st. between Howard and Eutau streets.
ROLSTON William, drayman, south Liberty street.
ROLLINGS John, Old Town, 57 Bridge street.
ROMIN --- , of St. Domingo, Alley between Light and Charles streets.
ROSE Joseph, carpenter, Old Town, 59 south High street.
ROSE George, cordwainer, Old Town, 22 French street.
ROSEL Charles, cordwainer, Old Town, Albermarle street.
ROSENSTEEL George, dry good shore, 139 Baltimore street.
ROSS William, dry good store, 9 Baltimore street.
ROSS John, merchant, store and counting house, lower end of M'Clure's wharf.
ROSS Ham, grain measurer, Waggon Alley, between Howard and Liberty streets.
ROSS Adam, baker, Fell's Point, West side of Bond street - upper end.
ROSS Robert, sea captain, Fell's Point, 9, Market street.
ROSS Ann, widow, seamstress, Old Town, 55, So. High street.
ROSS Ann, widow, mantua maker, Old Town, Jones's street.
ROSS John, silver smith, 65, Harrison street.
ROTHROCK Jacob, tinman, 13, No. Howard street.
ROUNDLY Francis, mariner, Fell's Piont, 28, Alisanna street.
ROUSE ---, ship carpenter, Fell's Point, Ann street - between Pitt and Alisanna streets.
ROUSSEAU Julien, sea captain, of St. Moningo - Alley between St Paul's Lane and Charles street.
ROUXEL jacques, of St. Domingo, 17, Charles street.
ROWAN Francis, waterman, Fell's Point, Strawberry Alley.
RUCKLE John & Paul, grocery store, 195, Baltimore street.
RUCKLE Paul, dwelling, 249, Baltimore street.
RUFF and CHAMBERS, ship chandlery, 18, Cheapside
RUGHEUR John, boat builder, Fell's Point, 50, Philpot street.
RUTH Hannah, widow, boarding house, Old Town, Jones's street.
RUSK John, butcher, Old Town, Albermarle street.
RUSSEL Rebecca, widow, West side of No. Liberty street.
RUSSELL John, drayman, Connowag street.
RUSSELL Richard, carpenter, Primrose Alley - between Light and Charles sts.
RUTH Peter, carpenter, Fell's Point - upper end of Bond street, West side.
RUTTER and ETTING, merchants, 96 Baltimore street.
RUTTER Richard, gold and silver smith, 87 Baltimore street.
RUTTER Solomon, sea captain, 5 Market Place.
RUTTER Richard, ship carpenter, Fell's Point, Strawberry Alley.
RUTTER and PARKER, wet and dry good store, Old Town, 23 Bridge street.

SABAH Augustin, of St. Domingo, Waggon Alley, West of Howard street.
SABLE John, ship carpenter, Fell's Point, George street.
SADLER Thomas, merchant, dwelling, 6 Water street.
SADLER Joseph, cordwainer, 60 No. Frederic street.
SAINSGASSIE Peter, of St. Domingo, No. Charles street.
SALMON George, Justice of the Peace, 118 Baltimore street.
SALMON John, merchant, dwelling, 4 Commerce street.
SAMPSON Joseph, Rigger, Fell's Point, Argyle Alley.
SAMPSON   , Fell's Point, 108 Bond street.
SANDS Robert, cordwainer, Forrest Lane.
SANDERS Linney, boarding house, McClelens Alley.
SANITTES Marie Joseph, of St. Domingo - Alley between Light and Charles sts.
SANKS Zachariah, carman, Barre street, Federal Hill.
SAUNDERS William, blacksmith, Old Town, Bridge street - beyond Winon street.

SAWYER Anthony, hair dresser, Fell's Point, 25 Thames street.
SAVOURY William, carpenter, Old Town, Front street adjoining English Church.
SCAGGS Thomas, cooper, German street - between Liberty and Howard streets.
SCHARFF William, carpenter, Old Tower, Bridge street - beyond Winon street.
SCHABER   , grocer, Primrose Alley - between Light and Charles streets.
SCHANY John, mariner, 110 Hanover street.
SCHARTZ Charles, dwelling, 30 Pratt street.
   Ditto   grocery store, 78 Charles street.
SCHRAEGLY Michael, inn keeper, Fell's Point, 8 George street.
SCHROEDER Henry, merchant, 167 Baltimore street.
SCHRODER Jacob, schoolmaster, So. Howard street.
SCHRIVER John, small beer brewer, 42 No. Liberty street.
SCHRYER Lewis, dwelling 50 Hanover street.
SCHULER John, labourer, So. side of Lexington street.
SCHUELER John, baker 26 No. Frederic street.
SCHUEMACKER Ignatius, lock smith, 39 Charles street.
SCHUMBERG Henry, drayman, south Liberty street.
SCOTT Luke, schoolmaster, So. side of Camdon street.
SCOTT Robert, bricklayer, Conawago street.
SCOTT William, wet and dry good store, Old Town, 34 Bridge st.
SCOTT William, dwelling, Old Town, 1 So. High street.
SCOTT Andrew, constable, Old Town, York street.
SCROGS Alexander, carpenter, Old Town,1 French street.
SEARS George, merchant, dwelling 67 Hanover street.
   Ditto   store and counting house, 9 Bowley's Wharf.
SEE Kamp Albert, merchant, 150 Baltimore street.
SEEMAN John, rope maker, 95 No. Howard street.
SEGAR George, mariner, Fell's Point, 6 Queen street.
SEGUIN Jean, of Cape Francois, 14 Commerce street.
SEGUY Margaret, widow, So. Frederic street.
SELLERS and SMITH, taylor's shop, 19 So. Calvert street.
SELLERS John, carpenter, So. Howard street.
SELLERS William, cabinet maker, Fell's Point, 13 Bond street.
SELLERS William, inn keeper, Fell's Point, Lancaster Alley.
SELLERS Abraham, taylor, dwelling, Lovely Lane.
SELLMAN Jonathan, shipchandler, Fell's Point, 4 Fell's street.
SENEY Joshua, judge of Baltimore county court, Paca street.
SENSNICK Joshua, currier, Boundary street.
SEWELL Thomas, cordwainer, Waggon Alley, between Howard and Liberty streets.
SHADE John, taylor, 34 So. Gay street.
SHAEFFER Baltzer, dry good store, 34 Baltimore street.
SHAEFFER George, dry good store, 16 Market Place.
SHAFFER Frederic and Co. bruss manufactory, 142 Baltimore st.
SHAFFER Frederic, brush maker, Gough street, near Fell's Point
SHALLY Adam, carpenter, 91 Pratt street.
SHALLY Jacob, carpenter, Eutau street. So.-of Baltimore street.
SHAMMOW Rose, widow, 56 Charles street.
SHANE Peter, drayman, 77 Pratt street.
SHANE Joseph, carpenter, Fell's Point, Ann street, between Pitt and Alisanna streets.
SHANNAMAN Abraham, carpenter, south Howard street.
SHARP William, innkeeper, 77 Water street.
SHARPER Jacob, barber, Fell's Point, 32 Fell's street.
SHARTLE Catharine, widow, sausage maker, Forrest Lane.
SHARTLE John, pump maker,   do.

SHAUN, Nicholas, bag maker, Paca street.
SHAW Joshua, eating house, Front street, west from Calvert street.
SHAW John, bricklayer, Eden street, near Old Town.
SHAW ARchibald, wharf builder, Fell's Point, 23 Wilks's street.
SHAW Agnes, widow, Old Town, No. Green street.
SHAW Robert, carman, Old Town, Bridge steet, beyond Winon street.
SHEARER Jacob, taylor, King George street, near Fell's Point.
SHEDDEN John, grocery store, 19 Water street.
SHEEN Henry, taylor, Old Town, Bridge street, beyond Winon street.
SHEERMAN Elizabeth, widow, seamstress, Old Town, Bridge street, beyond Winon street.
SHEETHOUR Henry, drayman, 44 Light street.
SHEHAN David, labourer, 43 No. Gay street.
SHEPPARD Moses, dwelling, 77 Hanover street.
SHEPPARD Thomas, store and taylor's shop, Fell's Point, 17 Bond street.
SHEPPARD Thomas, blacksmith, Old Town, south Green street.
SHERWOOD Philip, clerk, Fell's Point, Ann street.
SHIELDS Thomas, dry good store, 101 Baltimore street.
SHIELDS David, hatter, 14 No. Gay street.
SHIELDS Solomon, cordwainer, Fell's Point, 12 Bond street.
SHILLING Tobias, comb maker, Old Town, 47 French street.
SHILLINGSBERG Dolly, widow, Eden street, near Old Town.
SHIPLEY Richard, carpenter and joiner, Fayette street, between Howard and Eutau streets.
SHIVELY John, labourer, Fell's Point, west side of Bond street - upper end.
SHOCHOESY John, bargeman to the custom house, 16 Pratt street.
SHOCK George, biscuit baker, Primrose Alley, between Light & Charles streets.
SHOEMAKER ---, carpenter, Welcome Alley, Federal Hill.
SHOENBERGER John, taylor, No. Liberty street.
SHORP John, cedar cooper, 11 No. Howard street.
SHORT Dinah, washerwoman, Cow-pen Lane.
SHOTT Jacob, carpenter, German street, between Liberty and Howard streets.
SHRECK Didrick, comb maker, Old Town, Bridge street, beyond Winon street.
SHRIM John, cooper, 12 No. Frederic street.
SHROD Christopher, carpenter, Whiskey Alley, between Howard and Eutau streets.
SHRODE John, Butcher, German street, between Liberty and Howard streets.
SHRIVER, Jacob, brickmaker, Goodman street, Federal Hill.
SHRYOCK John, pump borer, Old Town, Pitt street.
SHULTZ John, harness maker, 17 No. Howard street.
SHOLTZ John, leather store, 89, Baltimore street.
SHURDIN Jacob, blacksmith, Fell's Point, Strawberry Alley.
SIBBER Martin, carpenter, Boundary street.
SIDENSTRICKER Daniel Frederic, carpenter, Old Town, Granby st.
SIDLER Matthias, tinman, Fayette, between Liberty and Howard streets.
SILVIA Francis segar maker, 48 No. Gay street.
SIMAND Henry, schoolmaster, Old Town, south Green street.
SIMELING John, inkeeper, south Howard street.
SIMMUND and CROOK, cabinet makers, south Frederic street.
SIMPSON Walter, lumber merchant, dwelling, 56 Hanover street.
SIMPSON Jane, widow, 53 Pratt street.
SINCLAIR Robert, carpenter, No. Side of Camdon street.
SINCLAIR Robert, waterman, Fell's Point, 3 Alisanna street.
SINGLETON William, cabinet maker, dwelling, 11 No. Gay street.
SINYARD Abraham, labourer, Old Town, Bridge street, beyond Winon street.
SITLER Abraham, dwelling, Fayette street, between Howard and Eutau streets.
    Ditto   oil and colour store, 19 Cheapside.

SKERETT David, revenue officer, Fell's Point, 57 Market street.
SKERETT Clement, inspector, Fell's Point, 32 Fleet street.
SKIPPER Thomas, carman, Old Town, 8 south High street.
SLADE Elizabeth, widow, boarding house, McClelen's Alley.
SLATER William, merchant, hardware store, 77 Baltimore street.
SLOAN James, boot and shoe factory, 5 Water street.
SLEPPY Jacob, carpenter, No. side of Lexington street.
SLUBEY Nicholas dwelling, Old Town, 11 Front street
SLUBEY Nicholas and Co. merchants, counting house, 42, Water street.
SMALL James, joiner, 7 Pratt street.
SMALL James, rigger, Fell's Point, Lancaster Alley, East of Bond street.
SMALL Jacob, physician, Fell's Point, 2 Shakespear's Alley.
SMALL Conrad, physician, Old Town, Albermarle street.
SMALLWOOD William, innkeeper, 36 Market Place.
SMITH James, cordwainer, 30 Baltimore street.
SMITH Peter, cooper and drum maker, 146 Baltimore street.
SMITH John, whip maker, shop, 203 Baltimore street.
    Ditto   dwelling, back of St. Paul's Lane.
SMITH William, merchant, dwelling 6 south Calvert street.
SMITH Robert, attorney at law, 8 south Calvert street.
SMITH Lambert, dwelling, 19 South street.
SMITH Thorowgood and Isaac, merchants, counting house, 31 Water street.
SMITH Thorowgood, dwelling, 33 Water street.
SMITH Samuel and John, merchants, counting house, 47 south Gay street.
SMITH Samuel, dwelling, 37 Water street.
SMITH James and Co. picture frame makers, gilders and carvers 6 south Gay st.
SMITH and BUCHANAN, merchants, counting house, 12 No. Gay st.
SMITH James, physician, 56 No. Gay street.
SMITH Casper, baker, 36 Light street.
SMITH Margaret, widow, 110 Hanover street - back.
SMITH John, innkeeper, 12 Market Place.
SMITH and NACE, flour and grocery store, 34 No. Howard street.
SMITH John Henry, printer and book binder 48 No. Liberty st.
SMITH Isaac, dwelling, East street, between Calvert street and St. Paul's
Lane.
SMITH Levi, labourer, Saratoga street.
SMITH Elizabeth, widow, innkeeper, Fell's Point, 59 Bond st.
SMITH Richard, sea captain, Fell's Point, 95 Bond street.
SMITH George, hatter, Fell's Point, 101 Bond street.
SMITH Thomas,   do.   do.
SMITH Christian, carpenter, Fell's Point - West side of Bond street - upper
end.
SMITH Philip, inn keeper, Fell's Point,   do.
SMITH Job, Justice of the Peace, Fell's Point, 1 Shakespear's Alley.
SMITH ---, sea captain, Fell's Point, Apple Alley.
SMITH Bazel, ship carpenter, Fell's Point, Apple Alley.
SMITH Cutlipp, rigger, Fell's Point, Ann street.
SMITH John, H:, carpenter and joiner, Fell's Point Strawberry Alley.
SMITH Daniel, ship carpenter, Fell's Point, 8 Fleet street.
SMITH Joseph, revenue officer, Old Town, Wapping street.
SMITH Adam, stage driver, Fell's Point, 35 Wilks street.
SMITH James, butcher, Old Town, No. East street.
SMITH John, starch and hair powder maker, Old Town, Hartford street, near
Stiger's lane.
SMITH Robert, mariner, Old Town, Stiger's lane.

SMITH Caleb, carpenter, King George street, near Fell's Point.
SMITH Job ship, bread baker, Fell's Point, 5 Bank street.
SMITH Isaac, shop keeper, Lombard street.
SMITH Mary, seamstress, south Liberty street.
SMITH Jacob, blacksmith, Boundary street.
SMITH Solomon, carpenter, 11 St. Paul's Lane.
SMITH Edward, taylor, dwelling, Lovely Lane, between Calvert and South sts.
SMITH James, innkeeper, upper Water street.
SMITH Jane, widow, washerwoman, upper Water street.
SMITH Eleanor, spinster, 41 Market place.
SMITH Tenence, plaisterer, south Frederic street.
SMITH James, innkeeper, 41 No. Howard street.
SMOTHERS Henry, labourer, Fell's Point, Alisanna street.
SMULL Peter, mariner, Alley between Light and Charles streets.
SNIDER Andrew, tinman, shop, 148 Baltimore street.
--- Ditto, dwelling, south Liberty street.
SNYDER Valentine, hack carriage keeper, So. Liberty street.
SNYDER John, ship carpenter, Fell's Point, 14 Fell's street.
SOLOMON Myer, dry good store 110 Baltimore street.
SOLOMON Isaac & Levy, hardware store, 112 Baltimore street.
SOLOMON George, drayman, 41 No. Gay street.
SOMERS James, huckster, Fell's Point, 23 Wilk's street.
SOMERS Eleanor, widow, Carolina street - near Fell's Point.
SOMERS Martin, cordwainer, 37 Harrison street.
SOMERS Daniel, baker, Old Town, Bridge st. beyond Winon st.
SOMERS Lawrence, merchant, 160 Baltimore street.
SOMERVELL & DUGUID, merchants, 88 Baltimore street.
SOMHALD Frederic, blacksmith, Fell's Point, 14 Wilk's street.
SOUTHWOOD Thomas, white washer, Dutch Alley - between Howard and Eutau streets.
SOWERS Samuel, printer, office and dwelling, Fayette street, between Howard
and Eutau streets.
SOWERVINE Peter, grocer, Baltimore street, between Eutau and Green streets.
SOYRE Marie Sophia, widow, Fell's Point, 70 Bond street.
SPALDING William, grocery store, 26 No. Howard street.
SPECK Henry, taylor and inn keeper, 2 Water street.
SPEED Lawrence, labourer, So. side Lexington street.
SPENCE John, taylor, Fell's Point, 13 Bond street.
      Ditto   do.   12 Fell's street.
SPENCER Benjamin, bricklayer, Fell's Point, 46 Wilk's street.
SPICER Samuel, carpenter, King George street - near Fell's Point.
SPOTWOOD Daniel, rope maker, Old Town, No. Winon street.
SPRY Ceasar, mariner, Old Town, North street.
SPRY Caleb, bricklayer, Brioy Alley, Federal Hill.
STACY William, cordwainer, Fell's Point, 18 Fleet street.
STACY Matthew, taylor, Second street - near the Falls.
STAHL George, taylor, Old Town, Stiger Lane.
STANLY Charles, merchant, 33 Baltimore street.
STANLY Mary, millener,   33 Baltimore street.
STANSBURY Daniel, carpenter, Fell's Point, 28 Fleet street.
STANSBURY Kizia, widow, inn keeper, south side, Lexington st.
STAPLETON Thomas, brush maker, 14 No. Frederic street.
STARK John, --- dwelling, 206 Baltimore street.
STARR William, taylor, Fell's Point, 5 George street.
STARR Obediah, sawyer, Old Town, North street.
ST. CLAIR George, sea captain, Fell's Point, 20 Shakespear's Alley.
STEEL John, merchant, 165 Baltimore street.

STEEL John, ship wright, Fell's Point, 19 Pitt street
STEEVER Levi,   ,Old Town, Duke street.
STEEVER Daniel, harness maker and trimmer, Old Town, North street
STEGEL Charlotte, widow, Old Town, 30 south High street.
STEIGER John, hatter, 250 Baltimore street.
STEIGER Mathias, carpenter, Paca street.
STEINBACK George, ---, 19 No. Frederic street.
STEMLAR Mary, widow, Lexington street, No. side.
STEPHENS James, ship carpenter, 80 Charles street.
STEPHENS Richard, sea captain, Fell's Point, 97 Bond street.
STEPHENSON Henry, physician, Lemmons Alley.
STERET Joseph, office, 49 Water street.
STEVENS Jane, huckster, 1 north Calvert street.
STEVENSON Moses, -------, Eutau street.
STEWART Archibald, merchant, store and counting house, 95 South street -
Bowley's Wharf.
--- Ditto   dwelling, 17 South street.
STEWART David & sons, merchants, counting house, 45 Water street.
--- Ditto   , dwelling, 29 south Gay street.
STEWART James, physician, 23 So. Gay street.
STEWART Richardson, nail maker, north Charles street, corner of Conowago st.
STEWART Charles, taylor, Conowago street.
STEWART James, sea captain, Fell's Point, 22 Thames street.
STEWART James, inn keeper and brass founder, Fell's Point, 2 Thames street.
STEWART Robert, stone cutter, Old Town, Duke street.
STEWART Hugh, bricklayer, Old Town, Duke street
STIGER Andrew, butcher, Boundary street.
STIGER Jacob, butcher, Boundary street
STILES George, sea captain, Fell's Point, 27 George street.
STILWELL John, hatter, Cyder Alley, south of Baltimroe street.
STERLING James, dry good store, 14 Baltimore street.
STITCHER Jacob, butcher, 25 No. Howard street.
ST. MARTIN --- , of St. Comingo, 47 Pratt street.
STOCKTON John, carpenter, Old Town, Bridge street - beyond Winon street.
STODDER David, ship wright, dwelling Fell's Point, 9 Philpot street.
STOFFLE ---, watchman and carman, Barre street - Federal Hill.
STOFFLEMAN Henry, joiner, Dutch Alley.- between Howard and Eutau streets.
STOKES Rachael, widow, bording house, Fell's Point, Ann st.
STONALL William, taylor, Fell's Point, 8 Thames street.
STONE John, inn keeper, Fell's Point, 4 Alisanna street.
ST. OLYMPE ---,of St. Domingo, 88 No. Howard street.
STOUFFER Henry, flour merchant, 15   do.
STOUT George, junr. grocery store, 188 Baltimore street.
STOW & ROSS, ship bread bakers, 96 Charles street.
STRAN John, sea captain, Fell's Point, 15 Alisanna street.
STRAWBRIDGE Abraham, carman, Old Town, 57 south High st.
STREET Daniel, labourer, Warren street, Federal Hill.
STRICKER John, merchant, store and counting house, 4 Bowley's Wharf.
    Ditto   dwelling, 15 Charles street.
STRUTTHOFF Barney, baker, 67 Harrison street.
STROWP John, turner, 62 Charles street.
STUMP John, merchant, dwelling, 55 Pratt street, store and counting house,
27 Cheapside.
STUPUY Peter, merchant, of St. Domingo, 10 Commerce street.
SUAU Amant, of St. Domingo, alley between Ligh & Charles street.

SUDDEN William, carpenter, Old Town, Bridge street - beyond Winon street.
SUCKLING Eleanor, seamstress, French alley.- between Charles and Sharp sts.
SULLIVAN Owen, carman, Fell's Point, East side of Bond street - upper end.
SULLIVAN Jonathan, dwelling, King George street.
SULTZER ---, butcher, Old Town, 29 Front street.
SUMMERS james Dent. schoolmaster, German street - between Hanover and Howard streets.
SUMWALD George, harness maker, 209 Baltimore street.
SUMWALT Godfrey, bricklayer, Eden street - near Jones's Fall's
SUMVALT Philip, grocer, 3 Second street.
SUABALDT Baltzer, --- , 94 Pratt street.
SUSANNAH ------, washerwoman, 10 No. Liberty street.
SUTTON Isaac, ship carpenter, Fell's Point, Apple.Alley.
SWAN John & Joseph, merchants, 121 Baltimore street.
SWAN Joseph, dwelling, 31 South street.
SWAIN Jeremiah, livery stable, Old Town, Granby street.
SWARM Samuel, carpenter and joiner, Old Town, 41 Bridge st.
SWEENY Mary, milliner, 49 Baltimore street.
SWEENY Richard, chair maker, Old Town, 71 Front street.
SWINGLE Peter, huckster, Old Town, 4 French street.
SYBERT Philip, carpenter, 77 Pratt street.

TANNER Pearce Lacy, dry good store, 21 Baltimore st.
TANNOCH James, cordwainer, German street - between Hanover and Howard streets.
TARE Catherine, widow, seamstress, Alley - between Light and Charles streets.
TAUSZ David, cordwainer, south Liberty street.
TAYLOR William, merchant, dwelling 7 south Calvert street.
    Ditto   store and counting house, 8 Bank street.
TAYLOR Robert, merchant, 2 south Calvert street.
TAYLOR John, mariner, Fell's Point - upper end of Market st.
TAYLOR Margaret, spinstress, Fell's Point, Argyle Alley.
TAYLOR Robert, schoolmaster, Old Town, Bridge street - beyond Winon street.
TAYLOR John, carpenter, at Nathan Garvins, Second street.
TEETS Gutlip, drayman, Fish street - near Griffiths Bridge.
TEVENER William, plaisterer, Honey alley, Federal Hill.
TEVIS Daniel, grocer, 16 No. Howard street.
THOMAS Andrew and Butler, booksellers, 180 Baltimore street.
THOMAS Paul, late vice consul of France, dwelling 216 Baltimore street.
THOMAS Paul, grocery store, 189 Baltimore street.
THOMAS John, dwelling and dry good store, Old Town, 17 Bridge street.
    Ditto   warehouse   do.   19   do.
THOMAS Joseph, inn keeper, Old Town, Jones street.
THOMAS John, --- , 31 Harrison street.
THOMAS Louis, inn keeper and grocer, 19 Light street.
THOMPSON John, inn keeper, 55 No. Gay street.
THOMPSON William, clock and watch maker, 55 No. Gay st.
THOMPSON Robert, labourer, 110 Hanover street - back.
THOMPSON William, schoolmaster, No. Liberty street.
THOMPSON William, carpenter, No. Charles street.
THOMPSON James, watch maker, Fell's Point, 4 Thames street.
    Ditto   dwelling   do.   16 Bond street.
THOMPSON Nathan, ship carpenter, Fell's Point, 2 Fell's street.
THOMPSON Robert, dry good store, Old Town, 14 Bridge st.
THOMPSON John, carpenter, Old Town, Albermarle street.
THOMPSON Robert, grocer, Fell's Point, 29 Wilk's street.
THOMPSON Alexander, carpenter, Brioy alley, Federal Hill.

THOMPSON Henry, painter, 71 Water street.
THOMPSON Hugh, merchant, dwelling, 20 No. Frederic street.
THORNBOROUGH Francis, sawyer, Fell's Point, 123 Bond street.
THORNBOROUGH Ann, widow, Barre street, Federal Hill.
THORNBURGH Joseph and Co. merchants, 186 Baltimore street.
THORNBURGH George, director of chimney sweeps, 211 Baltimore street.
THORNHILL Frederic, merchant, No. Charles street.
THORNHILL Robert, cordwainer, Old Town, No. Winon street.
THORPE Thomas, bricklayer, Saratoga street.
THRIMBLE Thomas, cooper, Fell's Point, 44 Bond street.
TIERNAN Luke, merchant, 155 Baltimore street.
TILYARD William, painter and glazier, upper Water street.
TIMMES John, joiner, Fell's Point, Strawberry alley.
TINBY Peter, huckster, Fell's Point, 75 Bond street
TINCHANT ---, of St. Domingo, Fayette - between Howard and Eutau streets.
TINGES Charles, watch and clock maker, shop, 62 Baltimore st.
    Ditto   dwelling,   Triplet's alley.
TINGES John, grocery store, 13 So. Howard street.
TINKER William,   , Fell's Point, 43 George street.
TINSEY John, taylor, Old Town, French street, Precincts.
TIPPET James, rigger dwelling, Fell's Point, 20 Philpot st.
    Ditto   rigging loft,   do. 36 Queen street.
TITTLE John, cordwainer, German street - between Liberty and Howard streets.
TODD Philip, cordwainer, Old Town, Bridge street - beyond Winon street.
TODD Elizabeth, widow, seamstress, 13 So. Howard street.
TOOL Catherine, huckster 75 Hanover street.
TOOL John, turpentine distiller, 26 So. Howard street.
TOOL Thomas,   do.   28   do.
TOMLINSON William, taylor, Fell's Point, 36 Fell's street.
TOMLINSON Joseph, saddler, Triplets alley.
TOMKINS Richard, mariner, Eden street - near Fell's Point.
TORBLE Peter, carpenter, 8o. Frederic street.
TORRENCE Charles dry good store, 21 BAltimore street.
TOWERS John, sea captain, Old Town, Albermarle street.
TOWNSEND Joseph, dry good store, 18 Baltimore street.
TOWNSEND Robert, constable, Fell's Point, 36 Bond street.
TOWSON Susannah, widow, 16 Commerce street.
TOWSON Abraham, mariner, Fell's Point, Wolf street.
TOWSON & BOURNE, dry good store, 93 Baltimore street.
TOY Joseph, bookseller and stationer, 127 Baltimore street.
    Ditto   dwelling   25 St. Paul's Lane.
TOY Isaac, umbrella and trunk maker, Fell's Point, 42 Thames street.
TOY James, inn keeper, 52 Market Place.
TRAVESSE Matthew, sea captain, Fell's Point, 29 George street.
TRENTON Anthony, captain of Norfolk packet, 60 Pratt street.
TREPANNY Augustin, carman, Fell's Point, Happy alley.
TREVAN & MAGLOIRE   of St. Domingo, Pratt street, between East and Paca sts.
TRICE Harman, hair dresser, shop, 23 So. Calvert street.
    Ditto   dwelling,   31 So. Gay street.
TRIALL Joshua, cook shop, Primrose alley - between Light and Charles streets.
TRIMBLE & CHANNEL, flour merchants, 92 No. Howard street.
TRIMBLE William, dry good store, Fell's Point, 3 Market st.
TRIPPE Edward, captain of Easton packet, 81 Hanover street.
TRITEL Jacob, shingle dresser, Fell's Point - upper end of Bond st.
TRUMBO John, carpenter, No. side of Lexington street.

TRUMBO Adam, carpenter, Forrest lane.
TRUMBO Elizabeth, widow, seamstress, alley between Light and Charles streets.
TSCHUDY Nicholas, grocery store, 166 Baltimore street.
TUDOR Elisha, carpenter, Fell's Point, 12 Wilk's street.
TULL Bridget, widow, boarding house, So. side of Second st.
TUMLY Henry, carpenter, Old Town, North street.
TURENNE John, ship carpenter, Fell's Point, 33 Philpot street.
TURNBULL Andrew, ship wright, Fell's Point, 24 Philpot st.
TURNER Nathan, taylor, Fell's Point, 29 George street.
TURNER ---, ship carpenter, Fell's Point, Ann street.
TUSLIN Septimus, coach maker, 13 Second street.
TUYAS Peter, carpenter, Fell's Point, 15 Philpot street.
TYSON Elisha, flour store, 49 Light street.
    Ditto   dwelling, 44 Hanover street.
TYSON Nathan, flour store, 51 Light street.
TYSON Jesse, flour store, 10 Bowley's Wharf.
    Ditto   dwelling, 25 Pratt street.

VALCK Andrian, merchant, dwelling, 62 Hanover street.
    Ditto   store and counting house, 77 Charles street.
VALETTE Charles, confectioner, 2 Market Place.
VANCE & BOYLE, dry good store, 30(?) So. Calvert street.
VAN BIBBER Abraham, dwelling, 97 Hanover street.
VANWICK William, dwelling, 30 so. Gay street.
VANWICK William and Co. auctioneers, vendue store, 22 Water street.
VEAL Pierce, bricklayer, Fell's Point, 16 Alisanna street.
VENNY Margaret, widow, Fell's Point, 25 George street.
VENO ---, 61 Harrison street.
VERO ---, Old Town, Albermarle street.
VICEROY Stephen, sea captain, Old Town, Pitt street.
VINCENT Samuel, clerk, 44 No. Gay street.
VON KAPFF B. and J. merchants, 202 Baltimore street.
VOUCHEZ John, merchant, 99 Hanover street.

UBRIC John, drayman, No. Liberty street - west side.
UHLER Philip, saddle and harness maker, shop, 11 Cheapside.
    Ditto   dwelling, 7 Bank street.
UHLER Erasmas, currier shop, 11 Cheapside.
    Ditto   dwelling, 47 Hanover street.
UNDERWOOD William, hack carriage keeper, Old Town, north Winon street.
UNDERWOOD John, hatter, alley between St. Paul's Lane and Calvert street.
USHER Thomas, merchant, dwelling, 190 Baltimore street.
    Ditto   dry good store, 192   do.
USHER John, dry good store, 161   do.
USHER Joseph, merchant, dwelling, Old Town, York street.

WAB Jacob, carpenter, No. side of Lexington street.
WALES and CLOPPER, merchants, store and counting house, 15 Bowley's Wharf.
WALKER Samuel, dry good store, 20 Baltimore street.
WALKER James L. painter and glazier, and oil and colour man, 124 Baltimore st.
WALKER Charles, sail maker, Fell's Point, 40 Market street.
WALKER William, sail maker, dwelling, Old Town, Jones street.
WALKER Robert, mariner, alley between Light, and Charles sts.
WALKASTER John, mariner, Old Town, North street.
WALL John, saddler and harness maker, 4 County wharf.
WALL John, retail shop, 37 north Howard street.
WALL Michael, taylor, 26 north Liberty street.

WALL George, carpenter, north side of Lexington street.
WALLACE and HART, merchants, store and counting house, 101 South street,
Bowley's wharf.
WALLACE Andrew, dwelling, So. side of Camdon street.
WALLCEE William, carpenter, Old Town, Low street.
WALRAVEN John, gold and silver smith, 119 Baltimore street.
WALSH Robert, merchant, 72 Baltimore street.
WALSH Catherine, widow, retail shop, Fell's Point, 27 Fell's st.
WALTER John, taylor, No. Liberty street, West side.
WALTER Peter, grocer, 43 No. Howard street.
WALTER philip, boarding house, 220 Baltimore street.
WALTON John, carpenter, 91 No. Howard street.
WARD Charles, merchant, store and counting house, 16 Bowley's Wharf.
    Ditto   dwelling, 43 So. Gay street.
WARD James, sea captain, Fell's Point, 18 Shakespear's Alley.
WARD William, sail maker, Fell's Point - Apple Alley.
WARD Thomas, sail maker, Fell's Point, 42 Alisanna street.
WARFIELD George F. and Co. grocery and flour store, 235 Baltimore street.
    Ditto dwelling, German street, between Howard and Eutau st.
WARK Ann, widow, seamstress, No. side of Bank street.
WARMINGHAM Richard, painter and glazier, 147 Baltimore street.
WARRELL William, carpenter, Old Town, Bridge street - beyond Winon street.
WATKINS William, blacksmith, So. side of Bank street.
WATERS James, grocery store, 86 Baltimore street.
WATERS James, merchant, dwelling, 80 No. Howard street.
WATERS Philip, flour merchant 82   do.
WATERS Martin, carpenter, Saratoga street
WATERS Hezekiah, dwelling, Fell's Point, 31 Thames street.
WATERS Hezekiah, wet and dry good store, Fell's Point, 33 Thames st.
WATERS Thomas, mill wright, Paca street.
WATERS Thomas, measurer of grain, So. Frederick street.
WATSON David, ship carpenter, Fell's Point, 47 Market street.
WATSON Thomas, rigger, Fell's Point, Happy Alley.
WATSON George, labourer, Goodman street, Federal Hill.
WEARY Thomas H. carpenter and joiner, Fell's Point, 5 Pitt st.
WEATHERBY William, cooper, Fell's Point, 15 Thames street.
    Ditto   do.   30   do.
WEATHERBURN John, clerk of the Branch Bank, Old Town, Granby street.
WEATHERSTRAND Thomas, cabinet maker, 16 No. Liberty street.
WEAVER Jacob, carpenter, No. side of Lexington street.
WEAVER John, block and pump maker, Fell's Point, 9 Fell's st.
WEAVER Margaret, widow, seamstress, Fell's Point, Lancaster Alley.
WEAVER Daniel, hatter, Old Town, 19 Front street.
WEAVER Caspar, painter and glazier, Paca street.
WEAVER Louis, blacksmith, 20 Light street.
WEAVER Susannah, widow, huckster, So. side of Camdon street.
WEBSTER William, carpenter and joiner, So. Liberty street.
WEEDON James, ship carpenter, Fell's Point, Wolf street.
WEHRLY George, carpenter, 9 Waggon Alley.
WEIR Joyce, widow, seamstress, Fell's Point, Alisanna street.
WEIR Charles, brass founder, So. side, Second street.
WEISS Felix gardiner, Old Town, Jones's street.
WELCH William, mariner, Fell's Point, Lancaster Alley.
WELCH Margaret, widow, shop keeper, Old Town, York street.
WELLMORE Rober, constable, Lombart street.
WELLMORE William, dry good shop, Lombart street.

WELLS Benjamin, inn keeper, Dutch Alley - between Howard and Liberty streets.
WELLS Mary, widow, 50 Charles street.
WELLS Cyprian, dry good store, 8 Pratt street.
WELSH Adam, tobacconist, 37 South street.
WELSH John, shoe and boot factory, 30 do.
WELSH and YONER, curriers, 10 Cheapside.
WELTNER Margaret, widow, Conway street, Federal Hill.
WERNER George, cordwainer, Old Town, So. Green street.
WESCOAT Lidia, widow, washerwoman, Fell's Point, 91 Bond st.
WESSELS John Frederic, clerk, No. side of Camdon street.
WEST James and Co.merchants, 174 Baltimore street.
WEST Thomas, ship carpenter, 110 Hanover street.
WEST Thomas, huckster, Hanover street, Federal Hill.
WEST Sarah, seamstress, Forrest Lane.
WEST Edward, rigger, Fell's Point, 58 Bond street.
WESTROM Andrew, painter and glazier, Old Town, 82 South High street.
WELLWOOD John, grocer, Old Town, 59 Bridge street.
WESTZ Jacob, shingle dresser, Old Town, North street.
WHEELER George, staymaker, 10 No. Calver street.
WHEELER Leonard, carpenter, 81 No. Howard street.
WHEELER Jacob, Old Town, Duke street.
WHEELER Isaac, labourer, do. do.
WHEELER Robert, bricklayer, Old Town, Wapping street.
WHEELER John, carman, Fell's Point, 16 Market street.
WHELAN Richard, grocery store, 132 Baltimore street.
WHITE and TAYLOR, grocery store, 12 County Wharf.
WHITE Oliver, grocer, 40 Charles street.
WHITE Joseph, sea captain, 46 Pratt street.
WHITE Simon, sea captain, 62 Pratt street.
WHITE Samuel, sea captain, Fell's Pint, 13 George street.
WHITE Francis,   Fell's Point, 18 Fleet street.
WHITE Griffith, carpenter, Fell's Point, 9 Wilks's street.
WHITE John, blacksmith, Old Town, Franch street - Precincts.
WHITE Thomas, labourer, back of East street, near St. Paul's Lane.
WIDNER Henry, hair dresser, 6 Harrison street.
WEISENHALL Andrew, physician, 40 No. Gay street.
WILEY Mary seamstress, Old Town, No. Winon street.
WILEY Mary, widow, Triplet's Alley.
WILEY George, boarding house, 38 So. Gay street.
WILINGMYRE Caspar, brickmaker, Fell's Point, Strawberry Alley.
WILKINS William, dry good store, 73 Baltimore street.
WILKINS Henry, physician and druggist, 23 South street.
WILKINSON and SMITH, cabinet makers, 16 Light street.
WILKINSON Joseph, taylor, Ruxton Lane - between Light and Charles streets.
WILLIAMS Ann, widow, dwelling and cooper's shop, 66 South st.
WILLIAMS and LOW, merchants, store and counting house, 88 Sou. street,
Bowley's wharf.
WILLIAMS Samuel, merchant, store and counting house, 10 Bowley's wharf.
WILLIAMS William, drayman, No. side of Lexington street.
WILLIAMS John, penny post man, Old Town, 60 So. High street.
WILLIAMS Charles, silk dyer and scowerer, Old Town, Jones's st.
WILLIAMS Benjamin, merchant, store and counting house, 3 Bowley's wharf.
WILLIAMS Christopher, sea captain, Montgomery street, Federal Hill.
WILLIAMS George, coachmaker, 71 Water street.
WILLIAMS Benjamin, dry good store, 5 So. Gay street.
WILLIAMS Mary, millener, 5 So. Gay street.

WILLIAMSON David, merchant, 69 Baltimore street.
WILLIAMSON Thomas, carpenter, Sarratoga street.
WILLIS Henry, dwelling, 32 Pratt street.
WILLSFORD George William, deputy sheriff, 34 No. Gay street.
WILLY Mary, widow, seamstress, Old Town, No. Winon street.
WILMANS Charles, merchant, dwelling 30 Water street.
WILMANS and WERHAGEN, store and counting house, 32 Water st.
WILMANS Catherine, Forrest street, Federal Hill
WILSON and MARIS, merchants, 105 Baltimore street.
WILSON James, dry good store, 178 Baltimore street.
WILSON ---, widow, dwelling, 13 So. Calvert street.
WILSON George, ship joiner, Fell's Point, 9 Pitt street.
WILSON Hugh, sea captain, Fell's Point, 39 Market street.
WILSON Jane, widow, Fell's Point, 17 Shakespear's Alley.
WILSON John, innkeeper, Fell's Point, 32 Philpot street.
WILSON John, rigger, Fell's Point, 24 Market street.
WILSON William, wood sawyer, Old Town, Bridge street, beyond Winon street.
WILSON David, carpenter, Old Town, 43 Front street.
WILSON David, sea captain, Old Town, Granby street.
WILSON Joseph, malster, Old Town, 41 French street.
WILSON John, bricklayer, Old Town, Wapping street.
WILSON Francis, confectioner, Ruxton Lane, betwwn Light and Charles streets.
WINAND I. taylor, 149 Baltimore street.
WINCHESTER David and Co. merchants, store and counting house, 71 Bowley's wharf.
WINCHESTER James, attorney at law, office, 12 No. Calvert street.
     Ditto   dwelling, East street, corner of St. Paul's Lane.
WINGATE Ambrose, carman, Welcome Alley, Federal Hill.
WINGATE Thomas, carman,   do.   do.
WINTERSCALE Thomas, Fell's Point, 38 Market Street.
WISEBAUGH John, carman, Fell's Point, 10 Alisanna street.
WILLS Sarah, schoolmistress, Triplet's Alley.
WOLF Philip, butcher, Dutch Alley, between Howard and Liberty streets.
WOOLSLEGER Jacob, painter and glazier, So. Liberty street.
WOOD William, merchant, store and counting house, McClure's wharf.
WOOD Leonard, ship carpenter, Fell's Point, 34 Market street.
WOOD John Rigby, drayman, Old Town, No. Green street.
WOODBERRY John, painter and glazier, Fell's Point 26 Bond st.
WOODS William, grocery store, 45 Baltimore street.
WOODS William, copper smith and tinman, 23 So. Calvert street.
WOODS Ann, huckster, 11 South street.
WOODS and ENSOR, merchants, store and counting house, 1 Bowley's Wharf.
WOODS Charles, carpenter, Old Town, Albermarle street.
WOODYEAR Edward, merchant, store and counting house, 30 Mc'Clure's Wharf.
     Ditto   dwelling, 66 Hanover street.
WOOLSEY Catherine, widow, boarding house, 3 So. Gay street.
WORKING Hanman,   Fayette street - between Howard and Eutau streets.
WORTHINGTON Henry, saddler and harness maker, Old Town, 25 Bridge street.
WOULDS Alexander, widow, retail shop, 94 No. Howard street.
WOYART Lewis, grocer, Old Town, Bridge street - beyond Winon street.
WRIGHT Grace, schoolmistress, 46 Light street.
WRIGHT Joshua, shoe maker, 63 No. Howard street.
WRIGHT Reuben, butcher, No. side of Lexington street.
WRIGHT William, constable, Fell's Point, 56 Bond street.
WRIGHT William, saddle tree maker, Old Town, French street, Precincts.
WRIGHT William, livery stable, East street.

WYANT Peter, inn keeper, 175 Baltimore street.
WYATT Thomas, labourer, Montgomery street, Federal Hill.
WISE William, sea captain, Fell's Point, Stawberry Alley.
WYTLER John, carpenter, Old Town, Albermarle street.

YATES and CAMPBELL, auctioneers, vendue store, 25 Baltimore street.
YATES John, merchant, 106 Baltimore street.
YEARLY Henry, ship carpenter, Fell's Point, 12 Shakespear's Alley.
YEIFER Frederic, grocery store, 66 Baltimore street.
YEIFER Englehard, merchant, dwelling, 24 No. Gay street.
   Ditto   wine store, 30   do.
YELLOTT Jeremiah, merchant, 10 South street.
YEM John, mariner, Fell's Point, 47 Bond street, back.
YONER Daniel, currier, 6 Cheapside.
YOULE James, cutler, Forrest Lane.
YOUNG Joseph, dwelling, 44 South street.
YOUNG John, sail maker, 5 Commerce street.
YOUNG Rebecca, widow, boarding house, 25 Commerce street.
YOUNG Cornelia, mantua maker, 26 Charles street.
YOUNG Nancy, boarding house, 2 No. Calvert street.
YOUNG Nicholas, cordwainer, Saratoga street.
YOUNG John, ship carpenter, Fell's Point, 39 Philpot Street.
YOUNG Mary, widow, boarding house, Fell's Point, 31 George st.
YOUNG John, carpenter, Old Town, duke street.
YOUNG Mary, widow, Lovely Lane - between Calvert and South streets.
YOUNG Alexander, cordwainer, 7 Second street.
YOUNG Jacob, cordwainer, Hill street, Federal Hill.
YUADT and BROWN, Printers of the Federal Gazette, Office, 3 No. Calvert st.
   Ditto. dwelling, East street - between Calvert & Gay streets.

ZELLERS Charles Henry, physician, 9 No. Liberty street.
ZEIGLER Francis, blacksmith, So. side of Camdon street.
ZIGLER Henry, cordwainer, Old Town, Bridge street - beyond Winon street.
ZIMMERMAN Henry, tobacconist, 35 No. Howard street.
ZOLLICOFFER John,   , 105 Hanover street.
ZOM Christian, carman, Old Town, So. Green street.

SUPPLEMENT   Omissions.

BARNABEU John B. consul of Spain for the state of Maryland, dwelling Brown's
tanyard, near Howard Park.
BARRY Redman, grocery store, Pratt st., between Franklin's Lane and South st.
BRADY Lawrence, huckster, Pratt street, between Franklin's Lane and South st.
DUSHAIL Etienne, consul of France, Smith's new buildings.
EVANS John, ship bread baker, bake house, Franklin's Lane.
FINLETTER Alexander, coachmaker, East street, near St. Paul's Lane.
HARRIS John, taylor, Old Town, 27 Bridge street.
MILLAR and BARKLIE, grocery store, 146 Baltimore street.
OGIER John, jeweller, Franklin's Lane.

                    Removals.

BULL James, cordwainer - to 30 Baltimore street.
KEATINGE, Henry, bookseller, binder and stationer - to 158 Baltimore street.
MOURIER Joseph, sea captain - to Fell's Point, Apple Alley.
NEALE John B. dry good store - to 33 Baltimore street.
PERIER Peter, taylor, to 37 Charles street.
PECHIN William, printer - to 15 Baltimore street.

BALTIMORE COUNTY NATURALIZATIONS, 1796 - 1803

extracted from the Baltimore County Naturalization Docket

March 1796
SMITH Abraham, Great Britain

March 15
CAUNE Felix, Rep. of France
MITTEN John, Great Britain
MILLER Robert, Great Britain
HATTEN James, Great Britain
BEATY John, Ireland
KIRK... Henry, Germany
SMITH Jacob, Germany
BITMORE Christopher, Germany
P... John Baptiste, Cap Francois
...(illegible)...
... Maglor(?)
... Garrett, Ireland
DEAS Joseph Lopez, France
BACKER Francis Helmig, United Prov.
Holland
WESSELS Frederich Francis, Germany,
Bishop of Munster in Westphalia
LATEURDAIS Joseph Auguste, S. Domingo
S. Domingo, France
THORNHILL Frederick, Great Britain

March 29
DUVALL Joseph Marie, France
HARANEDER Dominick Leon, France
RUCKLE John, Ireland
KONIG Henry, Hanover, Germany

March 30
FAUQUER Francis, St. Domingo,
Rep of France

March 31
SEGUIN Francis, Jr, St. Domingo,
Rep. of France
CARDENAND Edward, St. Domingo, Rep.
of France

September 1
de VILLARS Francis Didier Petet, Rep.
of France

September 2
CAMPBELL William, Ireland

September 3
GERARD August, St. Domingo, under
jurisdiction of Great Britain
STEINBACH Joachim Luburg, Germany,
Hamburg

November 21
MOULE Joseph, Great Britain
MOULE James, Great Britain
BUCKLEY Thomas, Great Britain

November 23
TUSH Michael, Germany

November 24
BRUNELOT Francis Bernarden, France
LAWRIE(?) Joseph, France
MURPHY John, Great Britain

November 25
SPENCER Robert, Great Britain
McCOMICK James, Great Britain
DeBUTTS James, Great Britain

November 28
ERENZEY James, Great Britain

November 30
BARRY Robert, Great Britain
CAMPBELL Joseph, Great Britain
CHATFIELD Joseph, Great Britain
HUDDELL ..., Great Britain
... ..., Holland
MILLER James, Great Britain
GOVERTZ Peter D., Germany
KOHL Burchard, Germany
SCHWARTZ August Jacob, Great Britain
KUPFF Bernard John Von, Germany
GROVERMAN Anthony, Duke of Odenburg

January 10, 1797
KING Benjamin, France
VEAL Pearce, Great Britain

January 11
McCORMICK James, Great Britain

January 12
LEMMON John, Great Britain

January 13
DAUGHERTY John, Great Britain

January 17
WHITEFEATHER Andrew, Great Britain
FITTERLING Jacob, Great Britain

March 15
GIBSON James, Great Britain
YOUNG William, Great Britain

March 16
CHAPEAU Anthony, Rep. of France
LEE George, Great Britain
USHER John, Ireland
ROE Alex Saunderson, Ireland
SOMERS Laurence, Ireland
NEALE John, Great Britain
PUNFIELD Samuel, Great Britain

BALTIMORE NATURALIZATIONS

March 18
MARSH William, Great Britain
... ..., Great Britain
... ...(two entries missing)...
MATTHEWS Patrick, Great Britain

March 20
GROSS John, France
HOSSEFROSS, George, France

March 21
CROOK George, Great Britain
MORROW William, Great Britain
GWYNN William of John, Great Britain
COULTER Alexander, Great Britain
DANES John, Great Britain
FULTON Alexr, Great Britain

March 22
PHASSE Peter, Germany
KENTER Charles Frederick, Germany

March 23
FREISE John Henry, Germany

March 24
TAYLOR Archibald, Great Britain
MAXWELL Robert, Great Britain
WOLFENDER John, Great Britain

March 25
WOLF Valentine, Germany

March 27
DANE Jean David, Rep. of France

March 29
COLMAN Joseph, Germany
DONOVAN Bartholomew, Great Britain

April 3
SHERLOCK John, Great Britain
LAWRENCE John, Great Britain

April 4
... John, Great Britain
... Mabel, Great Britain
...William, Great Britain
DELOHARY John, Ireland
NIEMEYER John Charles, Germany

April 5
HORNMILLER Jacob, Germany
COLLIN Andrew, Ireland
FOULDS James, Great Britain
HUNT James, Great Britain
MONDEL William, Great Britain

April 6
HOFFMAN William, Germany

CONDELL James, Ireland
BOOTH William, Ireland
HALLORAN William, Ireland
BURKE James, Ireland
COLLIER Robert, Great Britain

April 7
CALLAGHAN William, Great Britain

April 11
MARTIN Thomas, Great Britain

April 13
AMELUNG John Frederick Magnus, Hanover

April 14
FROLET Claude Joseph, France
LANNOY Louis Isaac, France
MARKER John, Hanover

June 7
KENNEDY William, Ireland
...(two entries missing)...
O'NEALL Bernard, Ireland
MARRAST John, France

August 11
SUIRE Edmand, France

August 14
GRAMBERG John, Germany

August 15
SHIELDS Peter, Prussia

August 16
VIBERT Amice, Great Britain
HEINECHE Frederick, Prussia

August 18
LACOMBE Mary, France
FITZE John, Great Britain
JONES Richard, Great Britain
FITZE William, Great Britain

August 19
ALBERTS John, Rep. of Holland
WELSH Martin, England
KONECHE John Godfrey, Hanover

August 21
MELVID David, Great Britain
GWYNN Robert, Great Britain
STEWART James, Great Britain
DAVIDSON Abraham, Great Britain
CARR Joseph, Great Britain
CARR Thomas, Great Britain

August 23
CARRICK Daniel, Great Britain
WERHAGEN Harman Conrad D., Rep. of
Bremen

LACAZE William, France

August 25
MALOY Edward, England
de SAINTE Simon, France

August 26
DWYER William, Ireland
BARRON John, Ireland

August 30
YOUNG William, England

September 2
GAMMELL David, England
KENNEDY John Fitzgerald, England

September 4
JACKSON Collin, England

September 5
CRAIGE Atcheson, England

September 6
LAW(LOW?) James, Ireland
LONG Kennedy, Ireland
KENNEY Alexander, Ireland
COLLINS Edward, Ireland
GRAY George Lewis, Ireland
VOLCHMAN Peter Adolph, Germany
FOCHE John Peter Frederick, Hanover

September 9
CULLODEN George, England
DENMADE Adam, England

November 6
BENNETT John, Germany
STULTZ(?) John, Germany
KROUSE Christian, Germany
HAHN John Adam, Prussia
TAYLOR Robert, Ireland
GALLOWAY William, England
McKAY John, England

November 8
KONIG Frederick, Elector of Hanover

November 9
MORTON John Andrews, England
LONG Henry, Ireland
SEETON John, Scotland

November 10
PURSE Thomas, England
BRADY John, England
SAVAGE Patrick, England
PROCTOR Jack, England
ASHWELL William, England

November 11
TENNER George, Germany
GARLAND James, England

JOHNSON James, England
CONNER Thomas, England
ALDWORTH Benja, England

November 13
HORNBY Gaulter, England
FARRELL James, England
FARRERHER, England
NANTY Henry, England

November 21
McINTIRE James, England
BELL Robert, England

November 22
WILSON Andrew, England
BENSON Peter, City of Hamburg

November 25
SULLIVAN John, England
LUTTIG John Christian, Prussia

November 27
SWEENY Elias, Great Britain
COCKRILL Thomas, Great Britain
STRIKE Nicholas, Great Britain

November 29
WHITNEY Thomas, Great Britain

November 30
HALL William, Great Britain

December 1
STEINBECK John G., Prussia

December 4
THOMPSON James, Great Britain
HAGAN Henry, Great Britain
ALBERS Lowder, Germany
ZWISLER James, Germany
McKIM Edward, Great Britain

December 5
SPANHOOFT Reinhard, Germany

December 6
REPP John, Germany
McTIER Alexander, Great Britain

December 7
ROBINSON James, Great Britain
CAMPBELL Hector, Great Britain

December 8
JACKSON William, Great Britain

December 9
HASLETT Alexander, Great Britain
DOYNE John, Great Britain
McINTIRE John, Great Britain

December 11
COURTENAY James, Great Britain
FROBOSE John Christian, Germany

BALTIMORE NATURALIZATIONS

December 12
DELOUBORT Louis, France
PRIEST Henry, Great Britain
STEVENSON William, Great Britain

December 14
WALTERS Henry, Germany

January 9, 1798
SHENEBERGER John, France
GROSS Lewis, France
WISE Felix, France
BOUGHMAN George, France
WISE Michael, France
HARDER Ignatius, France
HICKLEY Sebastian, France

January 10
LESAND John, France
REILY John, England
LIGGETT John, Ireland

January 11
ALLHAUSER John Earnest, Germany
CAPITO George, Germany
HEISLEN Thomas, Germany
KEILHOLTZ John, Germany

January 12
RAPP Deiterick, Prussia
SCHWERER Philip, Germany
DANEKER Charles, Germany
HIERY John, Germany
STRUTEOFF John, Germany
FEISBAUGH John Hunter, Germany
RAMSEY Robert, England

January 13
LEAKEY John, England

January 15
ERICKSON Barnet, Denmark
CAKEY Patrick, England
GRAHAM Robert, England
CLOTTES Peter, Germany

January 16
WAGGONER Valentine, Germany
WINN John, England
LOWERY John, England
PETERS John, Prussia
OLDFATHER Henry, Prussia
FITZSIMMONS Pearce, England

January 17
CAIRON Augustus, France

January 18
McQUIN William, England
DAGAN Patrick, England

January 19
MARTIN Hugh, England
FREDERICK Michael, Sr, French
FREDERICK Michael, Jr, French

January 20
FOLEY John, England
FOLEY John, England
FOLEY Timothy, England
KEAN Thomas, England

January 22
CROSDALE George, England
DARSY James, England
KELLY Patrick, England
O'BRYAN Charles, England
DARSY Michael, England
FAUNER Christian, Germany

January 23
FRIDAY John, Germany
CREAGH John, Ireland
WARMINGHAN Richard, England

January 24
CROSS Robert, England
CLARKE Henry, England

March 13
MALLORY John, England
HAMERSLEY Thomas, England

March 14
BARKLIE Thomas, England

March 15
POTHAIN (or Polhaine) Peter Francois,
France
KEPLER John T., Germany
CAMPAGNON Rene, France
SHOEMAKER Elgin, Elector of Hanover
KREBER Ruloph, Emperor of Germany
ROWLAND Thomas, England

March 16
STONEALL William, England
OSBURN John, England
ALCOCK Mansel, England
ALCOCK William, England
HARPER Samuel, England

March 19
RUCKLE Paul, England

March 20
MARTIN John, England

March 21
LEE James, England

March 22
BARRON William, England

CUMMING Thomas, England
RUCKLES Thomas, England

March 23
METTER Henry Leonard, Prussia
FLOYD Charles, England
PRESTON Wilham, England
CUMMINGS John, England

March 26
MESSONIER Henry, Prussia
CLARK James Harris, England
BUCHANAN Robert, England
O'CONNOR Michael, England
TOWERS James, England
DUNEY Michael, France

April 2
VALENTINE John, Prussia
HORN Christopher, Emperor (of Germany)

April 4
SPROSTON Samuel, England
GATES John, Germany
DUFFY Owen, England

April 5
O'CONNER Catharine, England

April 6
RUCKLES William, England
HIPWELL Humphrey, England

April 7
COOK William, England

April 9
STOREY John, England
ELVING William, England
KOLER Anthony, Germany
STEER (or Heer) John, Germany

April 11
SCHULTZ Christopher, Germany

April 12
CHABANNES Louise, France

April 14
WEBLING Charles, Germany
ANDOLLE Francis Andrew, Germany
McDERMOTT Henry, England

April 18
SWEENY Hugh, England

April 19
CONNELLY John, England

April 20
McCONNELL Thomas, England
ADAMS Alexander, England
BOLTE John, Germany

April 21
MACKIE George, England
HAND Moses, England
DUBOURG William Lewis Valentine,
France
THOMPSON John, Great Britain

August 16
ZACHARIE Ann, Great Britain

August 20
SCOTT Michael, Great Britain

August 21
ULRICK George, Germany
AULD William, Great Britain

August 22
HENRY John, Great Britain
JONES John, Great Britain
KELSOE Charles, Great Britain
FRITZ Joseph, Portugal

August 24
NAGLE Edward, England

August 25
MYLES Rebecca, England
BLOCK Simon, K. of Bohemia
GRUPY Francis, D. of Brunswick

August 30
FIRLEY John, England

September 4
HAMY Jacob, Germany

September 5
EISLEN Frederick, D. of Wirtemberg
McILLHENY George, Great Britain
CRAWFORD Andrew, Great Britain
HAISNEPE William, Great Britain
CATHELEN John Baptist, Great Britain

September 6
MATTHEWS James, Great Britain
LOGAN John, Ireland

September 7
MONDESIR John, France
BOOTH William, Great Britain
MORGAN William, Great Britain
JENNINGS James, Great Britain
McCLARY William, Ireland

September 8
DONNELLY Daniel, Ireland
MONTEETH John, Ireland

September 10
CLARKE John, Ireland
BOYD John, Ireland

BALTIMORE NATURALIZATIONS

September 11
KENTLEMEYER John, Germany
CORBET Dennis, England
FINLEY James, England
HERRON Robert, England
MAY Frederick, Rep. of Switzerland
CHARLES Robert, England
KAEFAL Nicholas, Germany

September 12
OVERGOSHT Adem, France

November 5
MITCHELL Peter, France
De CAUNDRY Peter Daniel, France
HARRION Joseph, France
LATOUCH James W., France

November 6
CAUSE Francis Bartholomew, France
HARSNEPE Matthew, England
Le COQ John, France
GROE John Anthony, France
HUISLER Anthony, Elec. of Bavaria
KONIG Levin Augustus Christopher,
Hanover

November 8
MARCHANT Peter Stephen, France
HERN William, England
ALLEGRE John Baptist Andrew, France
BRYNAN Edward, England
GUN Alexander, England
McDERMOTT Thomas, England

November 9
HANCOCK Joseph, England
LANDAIS Philip, France

November 10
PADUZE Peter, Emp. of Germany

November 19
TORRENCE James, Great Britain

November 21
FAY Robert, Great Britain

November 29
MACHANGER William, Great Britain

November 30
GEANTY Lewis, Rep. of France

December 1
CARREE Joseph, Rep. of France

December 8
ADONE Peter, Rep. of France
WADDLE William, England
ALEXANDER William, England
SMITH John, England

December 11
BARKER Thomas, England
FENNELL John, England
RUSSELL Charles, England

December 28
SCHWERTZER John Frederick, Elect. of
Hanover

January 14, 1799
REPP (or Jepp) John, Emp. of Germany

(The entries jump to June 1802)
June 1802
LAWRENCE Athelstan Dawson, Great Britain

June 13
GILLISON John P., Great Britain

June 14
KELLY John, Great Britain

June 15
SHARPNESS Simon, France

June 24
McNEAL Daniel, Great Britain
STEINBACK John A., Prussia

June 26
PAULY Daniel, Emp. of Germany
SCHNAUSSER George, Emp. of Germany
CONNER John, Great Britain

July 3
GUNDERMAN John Dederich, Elect. of
Hanover
WISEHAMBLE Christian, Prussia

July 6
SHAFFE John, Emp. of Germany

September 6
RYLAND William, England
CHILD Henry, England
BANNERMAN John, Scotland

November 15
O'NEILL Daniel, Great Britain

November 23
COCHRAN William G., Great Britain

November 24
LARSHE Heronimus, Emp. of Germany
FOSBINER Peter, Emp. of Germany

November 25
HAYS William, England

November 27
DETMORE Fred'k, Emp. of Germany
HOLMES Gab'l, Ireland

November 30
KERR Oliver, Ireland
RYAN Michael, Ireland

December 17
McCANN James, Ireland
NELSON John, Ireland

December 20
LEYPOLD Sam'l Fred'k, Germany
MEREFOLT John, Germany
DOBLER John, Germany
STREMMEL Fred'k, Germany
MacMANUS Owen, Ireland

December 22
TAEMBLER(?) Richard, Ireland

December 29
CULLIN Thomas, Ireland

December 30
CHEVALIER John Ab'm, France

December 31
MYER Charles John, Prussia
WILLIAMS Dutton, Ireland
McCAULEY Alex'r, Ireland
HUMPHRIES Carr, Ireland

January 1, 1803
McCORMICK William, Ireland
KANE John M., Ireland
ARMSTRONG James, Ireland
SCHWARTKIN August, Prussia

February 7
BRADY Sylvester, Ireland

February 8
HORN Philip, Emp. of Germany

February 9
GREGG John, Ireland

February 17
SELLERS James, Great Britain

February 19
LAWSON Robert, Great Britain

February 24
MILLER Conrad, Prince of Hesse

February 25
COLGATE Robert, England
CROCKETT George, England

March 3
ROGERS Robert, England

March 7
HOLLINS William, England

March 10
MYLES Jane, England

March 12
BOLTON Henry, Prussia

April 4
SEEMAN John D., Germany

April 6
RANKER John Henry, Hanover

April 9
ATTER (Atler) John, Prince of Hesse

April 11
PETERSON John, Denmark

April 12
JUDEN John, England

April 19
LEUYLE(?) Thomas, England

April 21
DESREMEASET Paulin Martin, France
DESREMEASET Philip Martin, France

June 9
SPELICY James, England
ZILMAN John, Germany

June 17
LEARY Timothy, Ireland
BONNEFIN Nicholas, France

June 20
WILSON John, England

June 21
GRICE Richard, England

July 1
ERWIN James, France

July 6
GUILDENER Charles, Germany

July 8
AYME Francis Samuel, France

July 12
ALLEN Samuel, Ireland

July 19
DAULCOURT Francis, Russia

July 20
POWELL John, Ireland

July 22
JOHNSON Matthew, England

November 7
ZEUMER Augustus, Prussia
CLARKE Joshua, Ireland
BOND James, Ireland

Index to

BALTIMORE NATURALIZATIONS

Last names unreadable

Garrett 59
John 60
Mabel 60
Maglor 59
William 60

ADAMS Alexander 63
ADONE Peter 64
ALBERS Lowder 61
ALBERTS John 60
ALCOCK Mansel 62;
William 62
ALDWORTH Benjamin 61
ALEXANDER William 64
ALLEGRE John Baptist
Andrew 64
ALLEN Samuel 65
ALLHAUSER John Earnest 62
AMELUNG John Frederick :
Magnus 60
ANDOLLE Francis Andrew 63
ARMSTRONG James 65
ASHWELL William 61
ATLER John 65
ATTER John 65
AULD William 63
AYME Francis Samuel 65

BACKER Francis Helmig 59
BANNERMAN John 64
BARKER Thomas 64
barklie Thomas 62
BARRON William 62
BARROW John 61
BARRY Robert 59
BEATY John 59
BELL Robert 61
BENNETT John 61
BENSON Peter 61
BITMORE Christopher 59
BLOCK Simon 63
BOLTE John 63
BOLTON Henry 65
BOND James 65
bonnefin Nicholas 65
BOOTH William 60, 63
BOUGHMAN George 62
BOYD John 63
BRADY John 61; Sylvester
65
BRUNELOT Francis Bernarden
59
BRYNAN Edward 64

BUCHANAN Robert 63
BUCKLEY Thomas 59
BURKE James 60

CAIRON Augustus 62
CAKEY Patrick 62
CALLAGHAN William 60
CAMPAGNON Rene 62
CAMPBELL Hector 61;
Joseph 59; William 59
CAPITO George 62
CARDENAND Edward 59
CARR Joseph 60; Thomas
60
CARREE Joseph 64
CARRICK Daniel 60
CATHELEN John Baptist 63
CAUNE Felix 59
CAUSE Francis Bartholomew
64
CHABANNES Louise 63
CHAPEAU Anthony 59
CHARLES Robert 64
CHATFIELD Joseph 59
CHEVALIER John Ab'm
CHILD Henry 64
CLARK James Harris 63
CLARKE Henry 62; John 63;
Joshua 65
CLOTTES Peter 62
COCHRAN William G. 64
COCKRILL Thomas 61
COLGATE Robert 65
COLLIER Robert 60
COLLIN Andrew 60
COLLINS Edward 61
COLMAN Joseph 60
CONDELL James 60
CONNELLY John 63
CONNER John 64; Thomas 61
COOK William 63
CORBET Dennis 64
COULTER Alexander 60
COURTENAY James 61
CRAIGE Atcheson 61
CRAWFORD Andrew 63
CREAGH John 62
CROCKETT George 65
CROOK George 60
CROSDALE George 62
CROSS Robert 62
CULLIN Thomas 65
CULLODEN George 61
CUMMING Thomas 63

CUMMINGS John 63

DAGAN Patrick 62
DANE Jean David 60
DANEKER Charles 62
DANES John 60
DARSY James 62; Michael
62
DAUGHERTY John 59
DAULCOURT Francis 65
DAVIDSON Abraham 60
DEAS Joseph Lopez 59
DEBUTTS James 59
DECAUNDRY Peter 64
DELOHARY John 60
DELOHARY John 60
DELOUBORT Louis 62
DENMADE Adam 61
DESAINTER Simon 61
DESREMEASET Paulin 65;
Philip 65
DETMORE Frederick 64
De VILLARS Francis :
Didier Petet 59
DOBLER John 65
DONNELLY Daniel 63
DONOVAN Bartholomew 60
DOYNE John 61
DUBOURH William Lewis
Valentine 63
DUFFY Owen 63
DUNEY Michael 63
DUVELL Joseph Marie 59
DWYER William 61

ELIAS Sweeny 61
ELVING William 63
ERENZEY James 59
ERICKSON Barnet 62
ERWIN James 65

FARRELL James 61
FARRERHER 61
FAUNER Christian 62
FAUQUER Francis 59
FAY Robert 64
FEISBAUGH John Hunter 62
FENNELL John 64
FINLEY James 64
FIRLEY John 63
FITTERLING Jacob 59
FITZE John 60; William 60
FITZSIMMONS Pearce 62
FLOYD Charles 63

-66-

Index to

BALTIMORE NATURALIZATIONS

www.ingramcontent.com/pod-product-compliance
Lightning Source LLC
LaVergne TN
LVHW061340060426
835511LV00014B/2024